GARLAND STUDIES IN ENTREPRENEURSHIP

edited by

STUART BRUCHEY
UNIVERSITY OF MAINE

A GARLAND SERIES

STRESSORS, BELIEFS AND COPING BEHAVIORS OF BLACK WOMEN ENTREPRENEURS

LOIS HARRY

GARLAND PUBLISHING, Inc.
New York & London / 1994

Library of Congress Cataloging-in-Publication Data

Harry, Lois, 1938–
    Stressors, beliefs and coping behaviors of black women
entrepreneurs / Lois Harry.
        p.   cm. — (Garland studies in entrepreneurship)
    Includes bibliographical references (p.   ) and index.
    ISBN 0–8153–1655–0 (alk. paper)
    1. Afro-American women executives—Psychology.   2. Afro-Ameri-
cans in business.   I. Title. II. Series.
HD6057.H37   1994
338'.04'08996073—dc20   93–49086
                                                                              CIP

Printed on acid-free, 250-year-life paper
Manufactured in the United States of America

Dedication

to my mother,
Ethel Mondy Harry Sheppard,
and to the memory of my father,
Eddie D. Harry

Table of Contents

Contents

Acknowledgments

This study could not have been accomplished without the help of my social support and technical assistance teams. I am thankful to my professors, family, colleagues, and friends for their encouragement, emotional support, and assistance during the development and completion of the original study and the revision of the study for publication.

I would like to thank the members of the planning committee, each of whom made a vital and unique contribution to the project. Dr. Wilbur Finch provided direction, expertise, and steadfast encouragement without which the study could never have been completed. Dr. John Davis contributed indispensable expertise on entrepreneurs and assisted in delineating the parameters, texture, and essence of the study. Dr. Jacqueline McCroskey's knowledge of research methods and attention to details enhanced the quality of the study. I wish to express my gratitude to Dr. Katherine Czesak for her consultation and editing. My thanks also to Mr. Clarence Henderson for his statistical consultation during various phases. I wish to acknowledge the assistance and encouragement of Dr. Helen Mendes and her invaluable feedback.

A special thanks to Joanne Wilkens, author of *Her Own Business* and President of the San Francisco Bay Area Business Women's Expo, Mary McDuffy, President of American Association of Black Women Entrepreneurs, and Frankie Jacobs Gillette, past President of the National Association of Negro Business and Professional Women, for their assistance in contacting their colleagues and encouraging their participation.

I wish to recognize three special African-American women entrepreneurs whose struggles, values, and accomplishments provided the inspiration for this study: my mother, Ethel Sheppard, her friend and colleague, Leathia Taylor, and my mentor and colleague, Dr. Verneice Thompson.

I am forever indebted to my daughters (Glenda Gabriel, Lenise Gibson and Lori Nassor-Covington) and my aunt, Arline Scott, for being my greatest fans and unfailing sources of candid feedback and emotional support. I also wish to acknowledge the comic relief and grounding provided by my six grandchildren.

And last, but not least, I wish to thank the members of my technical assistance and social support team without whom this project could not have been accomplished: Ed Bonner, Michael Quackenbush, Julia McCoy, Elaine Strickland, Glenda G. Gabriel, Janette E. Holman, Dr. LeVell Holmes, Helen Lewis, Virginia Phillips and family, Barbara and Wilbert Williams, Elaine Dawson, and Ruby L. Williams.

I

Introduction

This study explores the experiences of African-American women who own and operate their own businesses (African-American and black women are used interchangeably though this book). Black women have received the smallest rewards from their labors, although they have the longest and highest rates of labor market participation of all American women. This study examines the stressors they experience, the emotional and financial supports they receive and behaviors they use to cope with business problems.

The premise of this study is that differences in locus of control beliefs of black women entrepreneurs will affect their selections of coping behaviors and level of business success as they encounter business stressors. Locus of control is a psychological construct referring to individual's beliefs about their ability to control what happens in their lives. Of primary interest in this study is how black women entrepreneurs' beliefs about their ability to control their lives influence the types of coping behaviors they select and the successful resolution of business problems.

Black female entrepreneurs face numerous obstacles to their economic success. Their needs for economic guidance as well as personal and social support in their business enterprises have largely been ignored. Consequently, they have had to cope with the wide array of business problems faced by all entrepreneurs as well as those unique business problems of black women without training programs or business associations (Thompson, 1988;Wall Street Journal 12 February 1993). Although black women have played an important role in the American economy, only recently have their economic contributions or needs received public attention (Moses, 1985; Wallace, 1980).

Little is known about how black women entrepreneurs cope with the myriad and often conflicting roles and tasks with which they are confronted (Boyd, 1991; Brown, Goodwin, Hall, & Jackson-Lowman, 1985; Myers, 1980; Smith, 1981). Of most relevance to the current discussion is that little research has focused on the way in which black women function in the economic system or, more specifically, on black women as workers and entrepreneurs.

Only a few empirical studies in the fields of psychology and business have had a significant number of black women as subjects and most of those studies have failed to take into consideration the different psychological and environmental factors which have influenced African-American women's development (Latting & Zundel,1986; Sue, 1978). The standards used to examine psychological characteristics and business behavior have generally been developed from studies in which the subjects are white middle-class males and females (Brown, Goodwin, & Jackson-Lowman, 1985). There is seldom consideration as to whether or not those standards or operational measures are appropriate for groups of black women who have different cultural backgrounds and life experiences.

The primary focus of most previous studies about black women has been on the multiple and often conflicting responsibilities faced by black women in their familial and economic roles (Allen, 1979; Almquist, 1975; Harrison & Minor, 1982). In general, the treatment of black women in the social science literature has been characterized by distorted images which portray them as strong and long suffering, castrating and overpowering, or lacking in femininity (Gillespie, 1984; Staples, 1973; Harley & Terborg-Penn, 1978). In general, the American society has given a ready acceptance to the myths by which black women are typically portrayed, although there is little foundation for them in reality (Brown, Hall, & Jackson-Lowman, 1985; Sullivan & McCracken, 1988).

There is a wealth of research available which has studied coping behaviors among white entrepreneurial populations. There is no research, however, which specifically focuses on how black women entrepreneurs cope with stress. Much of the recent research on coping has found correlations among beliefs, past experiences, and resources, and coping behaviors (Billings & Moos, 1981; Folkman, 1984; Lazarus & Folkman, 1984; Pearlin & Schooler, 1978). It is to be expected that the correlations among beliefs and experiences will be maintained in the area of business behaviors and entrepreneurship. It can be estimated that the way in which black women entrepreneurs deal with business problems is determined by their belief structure, past exposure to similar problems, and their access to psychological and material resources. While this assumption is useful in developing hypotheses, the potential liabilities in generalizing from one population to another remain.

There ares six specific issues addressed in this study with predicted outcomes:

1. Black women entrepreneurs with an external locus of control will utilize more confronting, distancing, and escape avoidance as coping behaviors to a greater degree than black women entrepreneurs with an internal locus of control.

2. Black women entrepreneurs with an internal locus of control will utilize self control, social support, accepting responsibility, positive reappraisal, and planful problem solving as coping behaviors to a greater degree than black women entrepreneurs with an external locus of control.

3. Black women entrepreneurs with serious business problems will utilize self control, escape avoidance, and seeking sound support to a greater degree than subjects with less serious business problems.

4. Black women entrepreneurs with an internal locus of control will have fewer business problems than black women entrepreneurs with an external locus of control.

5. Black women entrepreneurs with an internal locus of control will derive a higher degree of satisfaction with their business than black women entrepreneurs with an external locus of control.

6. Black women entrepreneurs with an internal locus of control will have more positive resolutions of business problems than black women entrepreneurs with an external locus of control.

The research questions and hypotheses of this study on black female entrepreneurs are based on previous empirical research on coping and entrepreneurship. Most studies on coping have focused on medical, academic and life adjustment problems (Lazarus, 1982). Existing studies on entrepreneurs have dealt primarily with personal characteristics, venture capitalization, and business problems (Wortman, 1986). There have been very few studies of stress experienced by entrepreneurs (Churchill & Lewis, 1986), and no studies on the coping strategies employed by black women entrepreneurs.

If the environment for black women is different from that faced by the general population (in that their environment continues to be characterized by discrimination, poverty, sexism, and devaluation), they may require different locus of control beliefs and coping strategies in order to function effectively. To the degree that the most effective coping strategies can be identified, the current research should provide a practical base of knowledge upon which to base more accurate psycho-social assessments of clients and to develop guidelines for the selection of black women who might be viable candidates for entrepreneurship (Barbarin, 1983; Myers, 1980).

Entrepreneurship is an area of expanding economic opportunity for black women. While it is well known that small businesses have generated thousands and thousands of new jobs over the last decade, blacks have lagged behind other groups in starting and operating their own businesses. This is particularly true for black females (Hartman, 1985; Russell, 1984; Subira, 1986; Sullivan & McCracken, 1988). Despite the limited societal supports through training and financial programs, a growing number of black women are active participants in the free enterprise system as workers, managers, and business owners (Wallace, 1980; Washington Post, 12/28/86; Thompson, 1988). Business ownership can provide black women with a source of increased income and the opportunity to utilize the skills and knowledge they have developed at middle management levels. This encouraging trend, however, remains in its infancy, with only about 100,000 of 2.8 million female-owned American firms being owned by black women (Hisrich, 1986; Thompson, 1988).

Persons in the helping professions are often required to assess service needs and potential for employment of African American women as perquisites to their participation in programs designed to create economic self-sufficiency. Of particular interest to this study is the ability of social workers to assess, accurately, the potential of black female clients by enhanced knowledge of their labor market experiences and expanded information of the range of economic opportunities available, including self-employment. Their abilities to provide appropriate services are enhanced by understanding the interrelatedness of experiences, values, commitments, and coping behaviors of black women. Of particular importance, social workers would benefit by becoming aware of the complexity of locus of control beliefs and the multiple factors that influence coping strategies as such knowledge would enable them to offer guidance to clients in non-traditional careers as alternative routes to achieving economic success (Folkman, 1984). Currently, social workers, being largely women and working in agency settings, often adhere to traditional economic solutions that have been tried and found inadequate or unsatisfactory for a number of black women (Weick & Pope, 1988). Rather than trying to modify clients' beliefs or attitudes, social workers can develop the ability to assist black women in exploring careers in non-traditional occupations that are now viable for women.

The author's interest in conducting this study derived from an interest in exploring new areas of empowerment for black people from an interdisciplinary perspective. Social work as a profession is interested in economic self-sufficiency for many clients. It has become clear that training and rehabilitation programs for blacks have fallen far short of their goals (Marable, 1983; Willhelm, 1986). The economic needs of black clients go far beyond established services, and additional avenues for collaboration are needed. Social workers, who work in vocational rehabilitation, labor relations, private and public corporations, can benefit many black female clients by being aware of entrepreneurship as an alternative for some individuals. By starting their own businesses, black women may gain a level of economic self-sufficiency and security often not available elsewhere. Additionally, black women entrepreneurs can become a source of jobs for black men and women, as well as for other members of the labor force as entrepreneurial businesses continue to be the greatest source of new jobs and commercial development (Sexton & Smilor, 1986; Subira, 1986, Wall Street Journal 2/12/93). The current study, focusing on the personal characteristics and experiences of a particular sample of black female entrepreneurs, represents a natural outgrowth of this ongoing search for viable economic alternatives for African-American women.

This study is designed to test the influence of differences in locus of control beliefs on two important aspects of business management: (1) the coping behaviors used by black women entrepreneurs as they encounter business stressors and (2) the resultant level of their business success. The conceptual framework used is based primarily the cognitive theories of stress and coping developed by Richard

Lazarus (Lazarus, 1981; Lazarus & Launier, 1978; Lazarus & Folkman, 1984).

The four major categories of variables considered in the analysis are:

1. The nature of beliefs held by black women entrepreneurs regarding locus of control (internal versus external).

2. The relationship of beliefs held by black women entrepreneurs on the success of their business operations.

3. The relationship of the beliefs held by black women entrepreneurs concerning locus of control to the level of satisfaction derived from their business.

4. The relationship of beliefs held by black women entrepreneurs with respect to the types of coping behaviors utilized to manage business problems.

This study provides analysis of data on the experiences of black women who have started their own businesses. In addition, the data covers other relevant areas: the similarities and differences of the problems encountered by black women entrepreneurs as compared to other entrepreneurs; the types of financial and social support they received in starting and operating their business; how they actually coped with a specific business problems. Demographic data gathered in the course of this dissertation also serves to expand understanding of socioeconomic characteristics regarding black women who start businesses.

OVERVIEW

In order to develop an understanding of the environmental influences that shape the lives of black women entrepreneurs, Chapter 2 generally discusses the stressors faced by entrepreneurs and the special problems of black men and white entrepreneurs. It reviews the historical, social, and cultural environment of black women entrepreneurs. Additionally, this Chapter raises the question of how the different environmental experiences of these entrepreneurs influence their beliefs and coping behaviors. The Chapter reviews the literature on the theories of psychological stress, the cognitive theory of coping, and the role played by locus of control beliefs relative to coping behaviors.

Chapter 3 presents a systematic conceptual framework, which is used to derive testable hypotheses. Chapter 4 provides a detailed discussion of the study methodology, including hypotheses to be tested, instrumentation, procedures, and statistical procedures. Chapter 5 presents the findings of the study, including a profile of the sample, their business problems, and the results of the hypotheses tests. Finally, Chapter 6 consists of a discussion of the study results in light of previous research and limitations of the study. The book concludes with a discussion of the implications for both future research and social programs.

II

Literature Review of Stressors, Coping, and Black Women Entrepreneurs

This chapter seeks to understand the coping process as it relates to black women entrepreneurs by looking at the relationship among stressors, environment, locus of control, and experiences that individuals have. There is no clear understanding of the coping strategies utilized by black women entrepreneurs. Although coping concepts are quite central to contemporary theories of stress, attention to how persons cope with life's problems is quite recent and little is known about the specific coping processes individuals use (Moos & Billings, 1982; Pearlin & Schooler, 1982). Empirical research is still hampered by the multiple, competing, and incomplete conceptual theories of both psychological stress and coping (Menaghan, 1983).

In order to provide an appropriate background, this chapter begins with a discussion of the coping process. The next several sections detail stressors encountered by entrepreneurs. They are followed by a discussion of alternative definitions and empirical studies of coping.

CONCEPTS OF STRESSORS AND THE COPING PROCESS

In order to understand coping, it is necessary to understand stressors and the role that they play in the coping process. This section discusses of the various conceptions of stressors, the complexity of the coping response, how stress relates to coping, and the cognitive concept of coping that will be used in this study. In this study, any business problem is treated as a stressor which must be adequately managed by the entrepreneur.

There is no consensus on the definition of stress or as to how it affects a person. Many alternative theories and definitions of stress have been developed over the last three decades. Some of the better known include:

1. Stress is any nonspecific demand on the body, which may be either physical or mental (Selye, 1965, 1974, 1982).

2. Stress is any demand or event in the life of a person that requires change or adaptation (Holmes & Rahe, 1967).

3. Stress is a specific stimulus interacting with a specific organism which produces a reaction of stress (Appley & Trummell, 1967).

4. Stress is a process resulting from the interaction of three factors: the stressors, the mediator and the manifestations of stress (Pearlin, 1978, 1981).

5. Stress is the perception by the individual that a given event is one for which he or she lacks skill or experience with which to cope (Spielberger, 1972).

These diverse definitions conceptualize stress in many ways: as a stimulus, a process, and as an outcome of an experience. The definition of stress adopted for this study is that of Lazarus (1981), who defined stress as a transaction between individuals and the environment which is appraised as exceeding personal resources and as endangering well-being. In this study stress is treated as a stimulus and is equivalent to a stressor. Stress and stressor are used to mean the same thing throughout this dissertation and are used interchangeably.

In order to develop a better understanding of the many dimensions of stress, other models of stress also should be considered. Interest in studying stress began with concern about its negative physical impact. Originally, Selye (1965, 1974, 1982) was concerned with physiological reactions of stress and the medical aspects of being sick. He discovered that the body's initial reaction to the demands of the stressor is an alarm reaction, which results in specific chemical changes in the blood and tissues. Subsequently, an adaptation reaction occurs in which the body makes adjustments in order to cope more effectively with the stressor. Selye's understanding of stress has expanded as further research has shown that stress is a necessary (and potentially positive) part of life and can be generated by environmental, psychological, and social factors (Selye, 1974).

Another major emphasis in the study of stress has been concern with the number of stressful events which individuals experience within a short span of time. Holmes and Rahe (1967) began with the homeostasis mechanisms which exist throughout the body in order to maintain a steady temperature and other physiological balances. They theorized that any change is likely to be stressful to the body and argued that the overall impact of any change requiring adaptation is likely to be negative. To evaluate their theory empirically, Holmes and Rahe developed the Schedule of Recent Events (SRE), a self-administered questionnaire measuring the number of adaptive events experienced by an individual during the past year.

In all, five major conceptual frameworks for analyzing psychological and social stress have been identified (McGrath, 1980): (1) the cognitive approach, stressing rational process, (2) the experiential approach, focusing on prior experience with the stressor, (3) the negative experience theme (whether the person has been unsuccessful in managing similar events in the past), (4) the inverted V theme (the intensity of the environmental stimulation is seen as determining the degree of stress), and (5) the social interaction theme (which conceptualizes stress as originating in social demands on the individual).

In this study, the cognitive approach will be utilized. Cognitive theories are basically learning theories which seek to understand how humans manage their environment and build on experience. Cognitive theories bring together the thinking of philosophers, sociologists and psychologists. Cognitive process is called rational as it seeks to understand human being through reasoning or logical steps. Using a psychological basis, cognitive theorists attempt to explain why human beings are able to benefit individually and collectively from their experiences.

The cognitive methods were selected for this study as the psychological constructs being measured were developed by cognitive theorists. The constructs relate to the management of the environment by individuals and as such both speak to the coping process. And importantly, both constructs are quite fully developed, well known, and have been used to research similar populations.

Some of the first recognition of the importance of coping to the experience of psychological stress was empirical research conducted by the military during World War II (Lazarus, 1982). Psychologists had observed that brutal conditions led to breakdowns in the psychological functioning of some individuals, while others seemed to find ways to cope with the stress. By understanding these outcomes it could be possible to identifying the strategies for adapting to situations of extreme stress.

Cognitive theories are based on the observation that what differentiates human beings from other animals is their possession of language skills and their ability to think, reason, and solve problems (Werner, 1979). The evolution of gestures into language played a central role in the development of social relationships and interpersonal actions.

Cognitive experiences of individuals become part of their personal history through the psychological apparatus of the self. A rudimentary self is present at birth and develops from infancy through interaction with others and the environment (Kohut, 1977). The interaction of persons with others over a lifetime gives the self an identity and personality. These experiences of individuals influence the way they think, what they believe and how they feel about the world (Werner, 1979). Variation in experiences lead to variation in capabilities, beliefs, and vulnerability to stress (Kohut, 1971, 1977; Lazarus, 1981).

The recognition that there is considerable individual variation in response to stress was important to the development of cognitive theories of stress (Holroyd & Lazarus, 1982). These theories begin with the assumption that thinking and conscious reasoning has an effect on emotions, physical reactions, and behavior. The importance of the cognitive approach is that individuals learn how to deal with their environment by experiences and values. Some of these experiences and values produce ineffective and undesirable results, but since the ways that individuals handle their environment has been learned, they can be taught to be more effective and to cope in a manner to produce desired results (Lazarus, 1981, 1982).

The relationship between psychological stress and coping is a complex one. The definition adopted for this study is that coping follows the occurrence of a stressor and is an attempt to master or manage the stressful event that poses a threat to the individuals well-being. At the same time, one must recognize that the relationship between stress and coping is an interactive, ongoing, dynamic process. Coping is treated as a response to the appearance of a stressor which has meaning for the well-being or survival of the business.

Figure 1 provides a diagram of the complete coping process. This diagram was developed by the researcher and serves as an aide to understanding the literature reviewed in this chapter. Persons respond to a stimulus or stressor by appraising if the event is a threat to their well being. A secondary appraisal is made to confirm that the event is harmful and to psychologically review coping resources available to manage the event. The appraisals are followed by coping behaviors which may be either intrapsychic or actions (Lazarus, 1981; Lazarus & Folkman, 1984). An adaptation of this model of coping provides the conceptual underpinning for this study. The adaptation is discussed in detail in chapter 3.

Prior to reviewing the literature on coping, the stressors that our subjects might encounter will be discussed. The delineation of the various business problems experienced by black women entrepreneurs will assist us in understanding the importance of coping, the multiple facets of coping, and the relation of environmental factors to the stress and coping process. The next section covers three topics: entrepreneurship, problems generally encountered by entrepreneurs, and the special problems of black men and white women in starting and operating their businesses.

STRESSORS OF ENTREPRENEURS

The Nature of Entrepreneurship

Entrepreneurs take the risks, pursue the opportunities, fulfill needs and wants through innovation and starting businesses (Casson, 1982; Burch, 1986; Long, 1983). These persons are self-employed and take the financial burden of the success or failure of their enterprises (Brockhaus, 1980). According to Burch (1986) the essence of entrepreneurship is the initiation of change, either by developing new products or delivering services in a new or innovative manner. Entrepreneurship stimulates economic growth and development and in turn is stimulated by economic expansion (Casson, 1982; Burch, 1986; Drucker, 1985).

Entrepreneurship can serve several functions in a society. It provides a vehicle for individuals of low status, such as members of racial or religious minorities or recent immigrants, to offer goods and services when they have been excluded from employment or advancement in the established businesses (Casson, 1982; Hisrich, 1986; Sullivan & McCracken, 1988). In capitalistic societies, entrepreneurship makes it possible for individuals to achieve economic security and to gain access to power and status which are not available, otherwise (Burch, 1986).

Figure 1	Coping Process for Black Women Entrepreneurs	
	Examples of typical Stressors: Cash flow Credit/financing Lack of Management Skills Red tape Discrimination	
<u>Personal Factors</u> Commitments Religious beliefs Self confidence Need to achieve Locus of control	Primary Appraisal	<u>Environmental Fact rs</u> Family influences Sexism racism Social Class
<u>Coping Styles</u> Emotion focused: Denial Acceptance Externalizing blame Problem focused: Information seeking Flexible roles Direct/collaborative styles	Secondary Appraisal	<u>Coping Resources</u> Psychological: Problem solving skills Social skills Religious faith Social/Material: Family relations Colleagues / connections Financial assets Lines of credit
	Coping Behaviors Accepting responsibility Confrontive Distancing Escape avoidance Planful problem solving Positive reappraisal Self control Social support	
	Coping Outcomes Satisfactory Unsatisfactory Unresolved	

For the purposes of this study, to be an entrepreneur, individuals must be self-employed, take the financial risks of the success or failure of the venture, and control the enterprise with their judgement and commitment (Long, 1983). Some researchers define entrepreneurs as persons who create economic growth, or maximize profits through new combinations of business services; other researchers are satisfied if they just own the business and take the risks (Long, 1983; Casson, 1982; Drucker, 1985).

There has been tremendous growth in the number of entrepreneurs who have started businesses during the past decade, with an estimated increase of 81 percent in new incorporations (Casson, 1982; Burch, 1986; Freseman, 1984; Hartman, 1985; Russell, 1984). Some of the more rapidly growing economic sectors include high technology, health and educational services, and retail establishments (Russell, 1984).

Many of the new entrepreneurs were born in the post-World War II years and grew up during good economic times, enjoying the benefits of education, experience, and savings. Others are former middle managers, who chose to start their own businesses. Over half of large American corporations have cut middle management staff in the face of growing economic competition, de-regulation, the over-valued dollar, and take-over attempts (Freseman, 1985). Women represent an increasing proportion of new entrepreneurs, with three times more women becoming self-employed than men during the 1970s (Hisrich & O'Brien, 1981). By 1984, the number of women owning and operating businesses rose to 2.8 million (Hisrich, 1986).

Research has shown that entrepreneurs tend to be characterized by certain personality traits. For example, many entrepreneurs experienced difficulty fitting into existing organizations or bureaucracies (Burch, 1986; Casson, 1982). Feinberg's (1984) study of seventy-seven entrepreneurs found that they often feel unappreciated by their employers and dissatisfied with their jobs. Hornaday and Aboud (1971) in their study of sixty entrepreneurs found that they scored higher on he need for independence, achievement, and effectiveness in their leadership than men in general. Kets de Vries (1977) in his review of empirical studies on entrepreneurs found that the majority of them dislike routine, mediocrity, and inefficiency, and are almost always hard-working, goal- directed, and self-confident. Other studies by researchers have found that as a group entrepreneurs are creative, imaginative, and are constantly looking for ways to earn profits by delivering services or marketing products in new or different ways (Brodhaus, 1984; Burch, 1986; Casson, 1982; Feinberg, 1984; Kets de Vries, 1977, 1985; Casson, 1982). Also, they tend to be enthusiastic and optimistic persons, who are able to attract others and obtain their involvement in supporting the venture (Drucker, 1985).

Most entrepreneurs start businesses in fields in which they have had prior experience. They are likely to be highly skilled in what they do, and may have stronger technical skills than they do managerial expertise. Many small business owners are fond of stating that they attended the "college of hard knocks" (Larson & Chute 1978). They often insist on producing the same product in the same manner year after year even when sales continue to decrease. Not surprisingly, such self-made leaders may resent the advice of experts, consultants or professional managers.

Certain locus of control characteristics have been found to characterize the typical entrepreneur. Borland (1974) and Panday and Tewary (1979) found in their studies that having an internal locus of control was a factor in determining who is likely to become an entrepreneur. Locus of control is also related to the level of business activity. Miller's (1983) study of small and medium-sized business firms revealed a correlation between entrepreneurial activity and locus of control characteristics. Two significant studies on entrepreneurs found that having an internal locus of control and a high need to achieve are important predictors of successful entrepreneurship. Brockhaus (1980) found that successful entrepreneurs were much more likely to have an internal locus of control. The same personality patterns have been reported in samples of minority entrepreneurs by Durand and Shea (1974) in their study of black small business owners. Durand and Shea reported that an internal locus of control was associated with more business activity and larger businesses.

Locus of control has been found by researchers to be an important personal characteristic both in determining who will become an entrepreneur and predicting their level of business success. Therefore, it is expected that locus of control characteristics will be an important factor in relationship to black women entrepreneurs. Further, it is predicted that black women entrepreneurs will have similar locus of control characteristics as entrepreneurs in general.

The personal characteristics, values, and psychological needs of entrepreneurs (detailed earlier in this section) that drive them toward business ownership often have important functions in creating the situations that become stressors in their businesses that are listed in the section below.

Problems Faced by Entrepreneurs

Starting a new business is by definition a high-risk undertaking as fifty percent of new businesses fail in the first five years. The percentage of business failures rises to eighty percent within the first ten years (Hartman, 1985; Sullivan & McCracken, 1988; Wall Street Journal 2/19/93). Many factors contribute to this high failure rate, some internal to the business and others part of the broader environment.

Many of the causes of failure are within the businesses themselves. The entrepreneur may not have a clear concept of the business, as reflected in the failure to define the uniqueness of the business, the nature and scope of the market, and potential customers (Silver, 1983). Very few entrepreneurs start their business by doing a market survey, even though such a survey would tell them if there is demand for their product or service
and where marketing should be concentrated (Silver, 1983). Many businesses start without a written business plan, which handicaps the new entrepreneur from the very beginning. A lack of knowledge about such fundamentals as how long it will take to produce a product, how much capital is needed, and what level of sales are required to break even are all too common business problems that become stressors for many new entrepreneurs (Larson & Chute, 1978; Wall Street Journal 2/19/93).

Lack of operating capital and/or credit leads to many crises and business failures. The first task of any aspiring entrepreneur is to secure seed money to start up the business. If he or she lacks sufficient savings or personal assets, it is necessary to look elsewhere: common options include taking on a partner, securing funding from venture capitalists, or borrowing from financial institutions (Andrews, 1986; House Report 100-736). One problem with obtaining funding in this fashion is that investments are obtained only by giving up a portion of the ownership and possibly control of the business. The founder of the business may encounter difficulties in controlling the direction and structure of the business, since there is always a need to satisfy the desires of the investors.

Cash flow difficulties are likely to be encountered in most new businesses, creating problems in meeting current expenses for overhead, staff, and raw materials. The situation becomes even more serious when credit has not yet been established. Cash shortages also lead to an inability to invest in the research and development which is necessary to offer new products or services. This effectively prevents the new company from expanding its position in existing markets as well as exploring new markets (Andrews, 1986; Boyd, 1991).

Many new businesses are unable to secure sufficient sales to become and remain viable. Typically, the initial sales of the product or service are to family, friends, business colleagues, or contacts developed during previous employment. The next source of sales are usually referrals by satisfied customers drawn from known persons. Unfortunately, new entrepreneurs seldom utilize well-planned or systematic marketing strategies to expand sales. While it would be ideal for the new business to utilize an integrated strategy incorporating advertising, sales staff, and media exposure, this seldom occurs in the real world (Stephenson 1984).

New businesses are highly vulnerable to downturns in the economy. Inflationary trends may drive up the costs of doing business, while a recession can lead to postponement or cancellation of orders, worsened cash flow, and increased rates of bad debts from customers. In general, the small business is more vulnerable to fluctuations in environmental factors, e.g. shortages of raw materials, unavailability of skilled staff, and governmental regulations. In many cases, entrepreneurs cannot successfully cope with all of these threats, and as a result the business does not succeed (Gross, 1981; House Report 100-736).

Many entrepreneurial businesses have certain characteristics which practically guarantee that they will be prone to organizational problems (Crost, 1984; Richman, 1985; Aspaklaria, 1986; Burch, 1986). Often the problems can be traced back to the characteristics and psychological needs of the owners (Russell, 1984). During the start-up phase of the business, owners are involved in every area of the business, and management of the business is highly centralized out of necessity. For this reason, many entrepreneurs have a strong need to control all aspects of operations and to have the final say on all decisions, even after the business has grown to considerable size and worth (Feinberg, 1984). Excessively centralized businesses are characterized by management practices that create confusion for employees regarding job tasks, responsibilities and prerogatives. Operations in these businesses tend to be crisis driven as the employees devote much of their time checking with the boss or competing for power.

As a business grows in size, however, owners commonly expect employees to continue sharing a commitment to hard work and small rewards. Such expectations often create an environment of distrust, tight controls and employee turnover (Feinberg 1984, Ket de Vries, 1985; Crost, 1984). Key positions in small and growing businesses are typically held by the same individuals who have been with the business since it started, often relatives of the founder (Becker & Tillman, 1978; Boyd, 1991; Davis & Stearns, 1980; Grisante & Gumpert, 1982; Olm, 1985). As the business grows, delineation of responsibilities and delegation of authority become increasingly complex, and it is only a matter of time before more formal management procedures must be implemented (Burch, 1986; Casson, 1982; Crost, 1984). The inability of entrepreneurs to recognize this need and to make the necessary transition to a different style of management has led to many small business failures (Crost, 1984).

The owner is often in a quandary with regard to the need for more personnel. Increased volume might suggest a need for clerical support or professional staff, but careful analysis reveals that there is not enough regular work to justify adding full-time staff. At the same time, however, scheduling part-time staff may be equally problematic if customer contacts are a factor (Richman, 1985; Aspaklana, 1986). Alternate ways of managing uneven workload would be to hire temporary help or to contract out specific tasks. Entrepreneurs must decide whether particular tasks are best handled by staff employees or by contracting them out. Specific tasks which are not likely to be repeated may best be done by a consultant or outside contractor. However, the entrepreneur must weigh this benefit against the disadvantage that less control can be exercised over that particular facet of the business (Burch, 1986; Sexton & Smilor, 1986).

The availability of skilled staff is another problem. The small business owner has trouble attracting and keeping qualified personnel (Gasse & D'Amboise, 1981). Few small businesses have systematic recruitment and selection plans (McEvoy, 1983). In general, small companies suffer from higher rates of employee turnover than larger companies because professionals and managers with the requisite training and experience can often command a higher salary and better benefits with larger companies (Hartman, 1985; Gasse & D'Amboise, 1981). The best-qualified managers are likely to avoid small businesses, preferring instead to work for what they perceive to be more stable and larger corporations or to start up businesses of their own. Staffing problems, in turn, contribute to bottlenecks and uneven production (Gasse & D'Amboise, 1981; Hisrich, 1986).

Empirical research studies on entrepreneurs confirm the types and variety of business stresses experienced by small business operators. Gasse & Amboise's (1981) study of entrepreneurs of small manufacturing businesses noted that the owners are confronted with the problems of obtaining supplies, skilled workers, government regulations, and inadequate sales. High-tech entrepreneurs have problems with maintaining control of their businesses during periods of rapid growth and sudden drops in sales (Crost, 1984; Seglin, 1985). Starting a business requires long hours and hard work, and new entrepreneurs often find themselves isolated from family and social support (Boyd & Gumpert, 1983; Subira, 1986).

Since the problems listed in this section are common to white male entrepreneurs, it is to be expected that similar problems are experienced by most entrepreneurs including black women business operators. Information in this section serves as one of the guides in the collection of data from our subjects.

Black Entrepreneurs

In addition to the myriad of problems facing all entrepreneurs, black entrepreneurs have had problems unparalleled by any other group, including other racial minorities (Boyd, 1991; Cole, 1974; Sullivan & McCracken, 1988). It was not long ago that black entrepreneurs faced both legal and social barriers to the survival and success of their businesses (Johnson, 1985; Minkwitz, 1967; Marable, 1983;). As a result of the negative environment in which they existed, black businesses have remained small in number and size.

Historically, most black businesses have been in service fields and/or served the black community. These businesses were predominately small enterprises of sole proprietorship or partnerships, mostly operated by families. These businesses served as the backbone of black entrepreneurship and provided the major business role models and training available for black youngsters. Currently, many of the business operations in black neighborhoods are being purchased by other minorities (Dingle, 1985). When small businesses in the black community are not owned and operated by black persons, members of the black community are deprived of very important experiences for business participation, self-sufficiency, and economic cooperation. Instead, money leaves the community with each transaction, and few job opportunities for blacks are available (Dingle, 1985). The existence of black businesses with the full range of responsibilities and experiences is crucial to the growth and development of black entrepreneurs. Inadequate business experience is quoted as the primary reason for business failures (Stephenson, 1984; Snyder, Manz, & LaForge, 1984; Timmons, 1980; Wall Street Journal 2/19/93). The lack of opportunity for black persons to gain business know-how through either the wider society or neighborhood businesses (due to the decline in their numbers or changes in their ownership) exacerbates the rate of business failures among black entrepreneurs (Brown, 1986).

Until recent times, both the formal and informal social systems have operated to suppress the number of black persons who owned businesses. Black persons were not welcomed in business associations, professional groups, Chambers of Commerce, or other business networks until recently. Exclusion from these organizations deprived black entrepreneurs of important contacts, sources of information and knowledge, and financial backing. Without these important resources black business are certain to have difficulty, surviving, obtaining credit for financing, and achieving growth (Black Enterprise, 1980; Bailey, 1971). While the American society has used legislation, government regulations, and various types of support to facilitate majority businesses, the same level of supports were not forthcoming for black businesses (Kent, 1984; Stapleton, 1985). Prior to the creation of a special "set aside" program that reserved funds for minority business, only negligible numbers of government contracts were being awarded to black businesses (Marable, 1983).

The growth of black entrepreneurship has often not received support and encouragement from black family members, friends, neighbors, and community leaders (Subira, 1986). There have been important factors in shaping the anti-business attitudes held by many blacks today (Subira, 1986). Oppressed people always develop attitudes and beliefs to help them survive physically and to help them cope with their situation (Chestang, 1977). Before the Civil War, blacks owned and operated businesses in the South as well as the North, e.g. banks, retail stores, newspapers, and factories (Bailey, 1971). During Reconstruction and continuing until the middle of the twentieth century, brute force and coercion were used to destroy black businesses involving the loss of lives and the destruction of property (Minkwitz, 1967; Marable, 1983). These experiences helped to produce a survivalistic attitude among black persons (Minkwitz, 1967). More recently, the high rate of failure among small businesses opened by blacks in their communities have led many black people to conclude that entrepreneurship is not likely to succeed (Johnson, 1985; Boyd, 1991). Many black persona believe that there are greater rewards and security to be gained from salaried positions with majority businesses or as public employees (Marable, 1983). They fail to understand the role that these attitudes have in perpetuating the economic problems of black people in the United States (Marable, 1983; Subira, 1986).

One resulting problem is alienation which often exists between black customers and black business owners. Frequently, not only do customers think of black entrepreneurs as providing substandard services or products at higher prices than those offered by white competitors, but they also may expect discounts or special favors (Graves, 1982). Some older blacks remember the negative experiences they had in the days of segregation when they had no choice but to obtain services from poorly run hotels and restaurants

(Bailey, 1971). For whatever reasons, there often is a lack of patronage in the black community for black-owned businesses. Unfortunately, this sometimes includes the black middle class, professionals, and celebrities whose greater spending power and prestige are crucial to the success and survival of businesses (Graves, 1982). According to the *Wall Street Journal* (February 28, 1985) black businesses receive only seven percent of the income of black persons. Even in markets which were traditional strongholds for black business, such as hair care products, white companies were now receiving the majority of black dollars. Black people seem to be wary of involving themselves directly in efforts to improve the state of black businesses, instead choosing to get the most for their dollars. Black people have yet to accept the views of Derek Dingle (1985) that every ethnic group must have an economic base among its own people in order to be economically viable in America's capitalistic society.

Some of the problems in black entrepreneurship come from the weaknesses in the social and political institutions in the black communities. Cole (1974), Subira (1986), and Marable (1983) argue that the clergy and civil rights leaders, two of the most powerful forces in the black community, reinforce dysfunctional attitudes. For example, some preachers denounce the efforts individuals to improve their economic position through free enterprise, frequently connecting the growth of black businesses with the evils of money. Civil rights and other black leaders continue to expect the government and large white-owned corporations to provide jobs for black persons, despite the fact that economic growth in this country has been driven by small entrepreneurial companies for the past two decades (Casson, 1982; Burch, 1986; Subira, 1986). Subira (1986) says that while such messages may have been functional in years past, presently they serve to perpetuate defeatist and fatalistic attitudes and discourage black individuals from seeking economic independence through business ownership.

In his research, Subira (1986) found that the business practices and attitudes of some of the black business owners contribute to their lack of success. Both Bailey (1971) and Marable (1983) ascertained through their studies that many black business owners contribute to the problem by holding unrealistic attitudes toward their black customers. This type of owner expects black customers to automatically buy their products or use their services out of loyalty regardless of quality or price (Bailey, 1971). Some owners fail to establish systematic operations for soundness and expansion of their businesses and seem satisfied with being their own boss (Marable, 1983). Other black entrepreneurs lack the vision which is necessary to create large enterprises or nationwide corporations. They are content to make a profit and live comfortable lives rather than re-invest their earnings or profits. A number of black business owners limit their participation in business associations or networking activities to their immediate business interest, ignoring the promotion of larger black economic growth and development that may have greater impact for themselves as well as others (Subira, 1986).

This section on black entrepreneurs is focused on black males in business more than females. However, it is presumed that all of the special business problems that are encountered by black men due to discrimination, institutional racism, and class problems in the United States are also experienced by black businesswomen. These problems become stressors for black women business operators as they strive to start and operate new business ventures.

Women Entrepreneurs

Only recently has attention been focused on women as owners of businesses. Due to the limited number of articles on black women, this section utilizes the literature on women entrepreneurs, most of whom are white. Majority women and black entrepreneurs, whether men or women, have been handicapped by the dominance of white males in the American economy (Sexton & Smilor, 1986; House Report 100-736). There has been explosive growth in the numbers, types, and worth of businesses owned by white women. Whereas 2.8 million women owned their own businesses in 1984, only 100,000 of these businesses were owned by black women (Sexton & Smilor, 1986; Sullivan & McCracken, 1988; Thompson, 1988).

Minority and majority women share many of the same economic problems. Women and minority entrepreneurs are especially vulnerable to management and credit problems, and must constantly work to establish an image of credibility (Hisrich, 1981; House Report 100-736; Seglin, 1986; Wilkens, 1987). In addition, women have unique problem in starting and owning their own businesses, most of which can be traced back to pervasive social values.

Traditionally, women are expected to be dependent on men for their livelihood. Women have been expected to take care of the home and rear their children, unless there was an economic necessity for them to work outside of the home. Women have also been limited in educational and occupational opportunities available to them. They have found it difficult to obtain the necessary experience to build meaningful careers, as well. Women were long denied positions above the supervisory or middle management level (Hisrich, 1986; Hisrich & Brush, 1985). Thus, women faced societally based difficulties in starting and operating their own businesses because of their gender (Amott & Mattaei, 1991).

The institutional sexism of American society, and the resulting economic disadvantage, is demonstrated by the types of businesses operated and owned by women. Both black and white women tend to open businesses in the services and retail fields, which require greater time involvement of the owners and generate smaller receipts.

Although there are important differences in the experiences of black women entrepreneurs from white women business operators which are based on race, there are also important similarities in their experiences which are based on their commonality of their gender. Therefore, the problems that are generated by sexism that white women entrepreneurs have encountered are also predicted as stressors for black women entrepreneurs. It is to be expected that black women have experienced similar, if not greater, restrictions in their educational and business opportunities due to their sex. Black women will need to respond to the greater pressures of sexism by developing more variety and creative coping behaviors. However, given the multiple hardships that black women face it is unlikely that they will be able to overcome the restrictions that the society imposes on them. The businesses that are developed by black women are predicted to be in largely in the service fields that serve black people, families, and children.

Societal Factors of Black Women Entrepreneurs

The economic functioning of black women entrepreneurs and how they cope with the problems they encounter cannot be understood without reference to the historical, social, and cultural context of black women in American society. To develop a better understanding of the factors which shape black women's perceptions, it is important to consider social and cultural factors as well as individual-level characteristics. Socio-economic status and the nature of family supports are particularly important. Factors unique to black women will be discussed in this section. Although it is recognized that they share many experiences and values of other Americans, it is important that the problems of racial discrimination, sexism and class problems be seen as they relate to black women entrepreneurs.

Increasing numbers of professionals have come to the conclusion that many of the economic problems now being faced by black women may be traced directly to the structural discrimination and class conditions which have characterized American society (Amott & Mattaei, 1991; Marable, 1983; Burnham, 1985; Willhelm, 1986). Black women have been a part of the labor force longer than any other group of women (Moses, 1985). They numbered a quarter of a million unpaid slave laborers by 1790 in the fields, factories, and homes (Smith, E., 1985). The work they did ranged from the heaviest and the dirtiest to highly skilled and artistic. Slave women were used as industrial workers and worked under the worst conditions. They were often used instead of men to do the heavy dirty work in factories, foundries, mines, and canals because their labor costs were only two thirds that of men. They were fed less food and punished severely for small infractions (Smith, E., 1985). There were free black women during slavery in both the South and the North. These free women lived under the same social restrictions as slaves; however, there were a some free black women who operated their own businesses in both areas (Amott & Mattaei, 1991; Ledsock, 1984; Smith, E., 1985). They operated businesses as seamstresses, caterers, midwives, and washwomen (Moses, 1985).

Table 1 describes the Socio-Economic History of Black Women Entrepreneurs. The sections on family, social, education, and economic setting are shown in relationship to the jobs and businesses of black women for three periods in American history. Throughout each of these periods the businesses owned by black women have been in the service field, although technical and social changes have changed the character of those services. Table 1 was devised by the researcher based on data reported the studies by Ledsock (1984), Lykes (1983), Moses (1985), and Smith, E. (1985).

Until recently, American black women have been consistently relegated to low paying, low status jobs and occupations. They are still under-represented in all occupational categories except the lowest paid and the most menial positions (Amott & Mattaei, 1991; Disadvantaged Women, 1983; Dream Deferred, 1983). From the early 1900's when black women worked as farm laborers, semiskilled, and service workers to the 1970's when a third of them held clerical positions, black women have always been pushed into dead-end, low-paying jobs by the combined forces of racial discrimination and sexism (Moses, 1985; Rodgers-Rose, 1980; Smith, E., 1985; Wallace, 1980).

Table 1

SOCIO-ECONOMIC HISTORY OF BLACK WOMEN ENTREPRENEURS

	1800	1900-1950	1980
FAMILY	caretakers, chattel and unable to marry.	75% male headed households, wife work as needed.	55% male headed household, 45% single female heads & 67% poor.
SOCIAL	African customs and language destroyed, rigid caste system	legally or socially excluded from financial matters.	women's earnings necessary and sometimes sole support for household.
EDUCATION	segregated education in North and illegal to educate in South.	de facto or legally segregated/colle ge liberal arts excluded from technical or business.	more opportunity for training in professional, technical, and business areas.
JOBS	household/indus trial wkrs unpaid slave domestic and farm workers.	domestic wkrs, laborer or clerical wkrs, teacher, social worker.	clerical, professional, managers, laborers.
BUSINESS	wash women, seamstress, midwives, caterers and peddlers.	seamstresses, caterers or restaurants, beauty parlors, boarding houses.	retail sales, personal service, professional services, manufacturing, technical.
ECONOMIC SETTING	agrarian economy.	agrarian/manufa cturing economy.	high-tech, military, and industrial economy.

Numerous studies have documented the problems faced by black women in the labor market. They have not received the comparable benefits from job experience and higher levels of educational attainment that characterize less disadvantaged groups (Amott & Mattaei, 1991; Staples, 1973, Lewis, 1977; Wallace, 1980). In 1986, for example, black women held only six percent of managerial positions, and accounted for less than one percent of corporate officers in Fortune 1000 Companies (Black Enterprise, 1988). There are some social scientists that expect the labor market for black women to deteriorate further in the near future. According to them the information age of high technology will mean job shortages for all but the highly trained and the severe competition for jobs is likely to place black women at a further disadvantage (Murray & Harrison, 1981; Palmer, 1983; Willhelm, 1987). Some how most researchers and writer have managed to overlook the experiences of a small group of professional African-American women who have abandoned corporate jobs and formed their own enterprises. These black women seem to disprove the automative assumption that their businesses are unprofitable. Self-employment for this small group of black women entrepreneurs was found to be more profitable for than for white women according to 1980 Census Bureau data (Sullivan & McCracken, 1988).

Black women workers were 6 percent of the civilian labor force in 1978. They are expected to make up 10 percent of the labor force (13.9 million) by year 2000 (Wallace, 1980; Black Enterprise, 1988). Earnings by black women make up substantially more of the total income of black people than the income of white families (Brimmer, 1984). As there are now approximately 29 million black Americans, and this is expected to increase to 35 million by 2000, the importance of black women becoming more viable as entrepreneurs can not be minimized (Statistical Abstracts, 1988).

Black women entrepreneurs experience all of stressors encountered by each of the other groups of entrepreneurs, namely white men, white women, and black men. In addition, being the lowest status of the four, they have additional stressors which are unique to them. Whether black women entrepreneurs will be more influenced by the personality characteristics found to be important in selection and success of other entrepreneurs, the values and teachings of their families, or the historically influences of their race and gender is an interesting question. However, the purpose of this study is to learn how locus of control beliefs affects the functioning of black women who become entrepreneurs. We may learn that the experiences of black women entrepreneurs which are determined by societal factors of race, gender and class have created different locus of control beliefs. These differences may be functional for black women as they live their lives and operate their businesses.

EMPIRICAL STUDIES ON COPING

Definition of Coping

The occurrence of stressors, individual appraisals, and the subsequent adoption of specific coping behaviors should be seen as a dynamic process. Only when an event is appraised as representing a threat does coping occur (Lazarus, 1982). Both the original appraisal of an event as threatening or non-threatening and the specific coping behavior chosen are a function of beliefs which have developed over the course of an individual's life.

The term "coping" has been widely used in recent years. The specific meaning of the term has become somewhat blurred. Many researchers conceptualize coping as an umbrella term (Menaghan, 1983; Rutter, 1983), to facilitate understanding and acceptance by the general public (Haggerty, 1983). The present level of empirical research on coping remains very basic (Fleishman, 1984). Researchers in the social sciences have been unable to reach a consensus on the precise definition of coping. In fact, it has only been in recent years that coping strategies have been systematically and scientifically studied (Pearlin & Schooler, 1978).

In this dissertation, coping is defined as any effort, psychological, physical, or behavioral to manage a stressor. Psychological coping may involves thinking, planning, evaluating, or palliative measures to manage the environment. Physical coping involves any changes that take place in the body to adjust to the demands of stress. Behavioral coping is engaging in conscious efforts and activities to improve a stressful situation (Pelletier, 1982; Lazarus & Folkman, 1984).

Individual interactions with (and attempts to manage) the surrounding environment have long been a concern of psychologists with diverse theoretical orientations. Not surprisingly, the theoretical explanations differ considerably. Psychoanalytic theories and ego psychology use the concept of conflict resolution to explain those ego processes which mediate between the person's impulses and the constraints of external reality. Developmental psychology focuses on the accumulation of coping abilities and resources which develop over the life span and provide individuals with the ability to handle problems during each stage of the life cycle. Evolutionary and behavioral approaches emphasize the problem solving aspects of coping to explain how individuals cope with problems they encounter (Moos & Billings, 1982).

Coping takes places in many contexts, and its multi-dimensionality must be recognized. At one level, coping is a dynamic cognitive process which occurs in the interaction of individual with environment. However, coping also involves psychological, physiological, behavioral, and social components (Menaghan 1983; Pearlin & Schooler, 1978; Lazarus & Folkman, 1984). Coping has a significant social dimension as much of the stress experienced by individuals originates in their social roles. Individuals typically cope by making adjustments in relationships and role performance (Pearlin & Schooler, 1978).

Coping has been interpreted in many ways, e.g. mastery, defenses, and adaptation. Selye observed that a stressor may be followed by physical and chemical changes in the body. Exposure to prolonged psychological and emotional stressors may be result in physical illness (Pelletier, 1979). Physical coping involves both voluntary and involuntary changes in the body to manage the effects of stress (Selye, 1956, 1974). Examples of physical coping include relaxation exercises and specific tasks intended to improve the situation (Pelletier, 1982; Folkman & Larzarus, 1985, 1986).

Some well-known alternative definitions of coping include:

1. An attempt to master a new situation that can be potentially threatening, frustrating, challenging, or gratifying (Murphy and Moriarity, 1976).

2. Overt and covert behaviors that are taken to reduce or eliminate psychological distress or stressful conditions (Fleishman, 1984).

3. As essentially any response to external life strains that serves to prevent, avoid, or control emotional distress (Pearlin & Schooler, 1978).

4. As constantly changing cognitive and behavioral efforts to manage specific external and or internal demands that are

appraised as threatening or exceeding the resources of the person (Lazarus & Folkman, 1984).

Coping was originally seen as a problem solving effort which occurs when individuals face stressors which are directly related to their welfare and which are taxing to their adaptive ability (Lazarus, Averill & Opton, 1974). Lazarus and Launier (1978) further defined coping efforts as having both action-oriented and intrapsychic components. Both cognitive and behavioral coping are important as the individual seeks to master, tolerate, or reduce external and/or internal demands and conflicts (Folkman & Lazarus, 1980). More recently, the dynamic nature of coping behaviors, both cognitive and behavioral, has become the focus of attention (Lazarus & Folkman, 1984). The primary dimensions of cognitive coping include coping styles (generalized attitudes, values, and skills), appraisals (intrapsychic evaluations of events), and coping behaviors (problem-solving or palliative adjustments of emotional reactions). Most researchers have incorporated these basic dimensions into their conceptual frameworks, although terminology may differ from study to study.

Lazarus' (1981) approach seeks to explain individual variation by focusing on how cognitive processes shape emotions. What a person thinks is shaped by beliefs, values, commitments, skills, and physical constitution. These factors are different for each person and results in different conclusions and views that serve as the foundation for the coping process. Individuals' views become part of a dynamic transactional process which includes the individual, the environment, and particular events or situations. These views come in at the point of appraisal; they influence the original decision as to whether an event is important in its specific context and evaluate whether it is necessary to generate a coping effort.

Research Findings

Studies on coping of various subjects range from looking broadly at individual differences to comparison between groups. The studies discussed below are listed because they contribute to the body of knowledge that exists on coping with psychological stress. Although an insufficient number of black women were included as subjects to be reported separately, the findings can be used as guidelines in developing hypotheses for this study.

A number of research studies have examined the coping behavior of black people in relationship to stressors and the resultant levels of their psychological distress. Neff (1985) studied 829 Florida residents and reported that there were no significant differences in the levels distress between blacks and whites over changes in their lives, even though the blacks in the study were clearly socioeconomically disadvantaged. Neff pointed out that the unavailability of the regular social and material coping resources forces blacks to adopt a coping style of blaming the system or accepting the situation as fate. Neff's study results are consistent with Barbarin (1983) and Chestang (1984) who have found that oppressed people rely on alternate explanations of the world to help them feel better about that which they cannot change. Foster and Perry (1982) studied 286 Detroit blacks, and found that positive self-evaluations were based on satisfaction with personal and family life rather than environmental circumstances.

Barbarin's (1983) study of black families' coping with seriously ill children used the Lazarus cognitive model. Barbarin reported certain factors that influenced the appraisal of threats in black families which were different from white families. Black families included additional factors relating to their race, social status, and beliefs about fate in the appraisals of their situations. His findings revealed that in difficult situation they relied heavily on emotion-focused coping responses which were largely characterized by religious beliefs and the externalizing of blame.

Empirical research has produced mixed results on gender differences in coping. Some studies have shown differences in coping patterns between males and females (Fleishman, 1984). Men have been were found to use more problem focused coping, while women tend to use more emotional focused coping behaviors (Pearlin & Schooler, 1978). However, Folkman and Lazarus (1980) found no gender differences on either appraisals or coping behaviors.

Kobasa (1983) studied a sample of telephone company executives and found considerable individual variation in coping responses to similar stressors (1983). Certain executives were found to utilize more positive and effective coping behaviors; they exhibited characteristics of being fully committed to what they were doing, having a sense of control over events, and considering change as normal. Kobasa referred to these traits as hardiness, and argued that they served as protectors of both mental and physical health against stressful life events, even when controlling for demographic or ethnic variables.

Several studies which have included black women entrepreneurs among their subjects do not provide specific information regarding the black women: the problems they encounter, how they cope with them, or even their personal characteristics. DeCarlo and Lyons (1979) and Hisrich and Brush (1985) included black women as subjects when they compared minorities with white women. However, the number of black women was not specified and the findings for them were not reported separately. Gaston (1980) used black women entrepreneurs as subjects, but focused entirely on personal relations with their husbands. In general, the literature fails to provide an adequate base of knowledge regarding the way in which black women entrepreneurs cope with business problems.

Coping by Black Women

While the literature on black women tells us something about what types of problems they have faced and what they have done about them, there is little information regarding their psychological make up (Brown, Goodwin, Hall, & Jackson-Lowmn, 1985). Some general ideas about the beliefs of black women can be inferred from fiction, nonfiction, and academic writings. Discrimination, racism, economic hardship, and family problems are all stressors with which black women must cope. Many of these stressors are structural problems and beyond the scope of individual control. Many anecdotal stories on black women have been credited with a superior ability to survive and endure such problems (Gillespie, 1984).

The few existing empirical studies on coping by black women demonstrate that they have established creative and imaginative strategies for managing multiple societal, economic, and familial problems (Adams, 1983; Epstein, 1973; Moses, 1985; Myers, 1980). Epstein (1973) and Smith (1982) found that black women were socialized to handle multiple roles, and that they were expected to continue working following marriage and childbirth. Myers (1980) studied the coping behaviors of black women in Mississippi and Michigan. They found that exposure to role models influenced the development of the predominant attitude among black women that they could handle a large number of roles. They relied on relatives and friends as sources of both inspiration and social support. These findings were supported by Mays (1985), who found that black

women were the strongest supporters of each other regardless of
status or occupational differences.

Coping with multiple responsibilities without question can lead
to the problem of role overload. Harrison & Minor(1982) found that
married black women with young children were vulnerable to physical
and emotional problems. This was particularly true when they
encountered difficulties in prioritizing or reducing role demands.

Black women experience some of their greatest stress in the work
environment (Almquist, 1975; Moses, 1985; Smith, E., 1985). Lykes'
(1983), in a retrospective study of elderly black women, reported that
many of them were assertive and creative in challenging
discrimination and mistreatment experienced on the job. These
women used both direct coping (e.g. challenging the treatment they
received) and emotional coping (e.g. talking problems over with
coworkers and friends).

Burlew (1982) found black women in non-traditional fields were
socially isolated and limited in their career opportunities. They coped
with these problems by marrying lower status men and by relying on
family and friends for social support. Black professional women
coped with the labor market problems by seeking out protected work
settings such as large bureaucracies, black community agencies, and
self-employment (Epstein, 1973; Gilkes, 1982; Smith, E., 1985). As
pointed out by Griffin (19&6), who conducted a study on the
experiences of black women as authority figures in mixed racial
groups, it may not always be possible to satisfactorily resolve the
problems encountered on the job.

The literature on stressors, locus of control beliefs, and coping
efforts form the basis for the conceptual framework and research
hypotheses of this study. However, it was also necessary to rely on
the literature on black women in such fields as sociology and black
studies. Since there have been no studies on locus of control and
coping by black women entrepreneurs, previous empirical studies
using the same psychological constructs and similar subjects were
used as general guidelines.

CHAPTER SUMMARY

This chapter reviewed important theories and studies in several relevant areas. The discussion of theories of stress was brief, but necessary in order to provide the appropriate context for the discussion of appraisal and coping processes. The section was followed by a lengthy discussion of stressors that are encountered by various categories of entrepreneurs and black women. The section on coping emphasized the cognitive approaches of Lazarus and his colleagues as providing an appropriate framework for understanding how black women entrepreneurs actually cope. Locus of control was also discussed with significance of the concept to understanding entrepreneurial behavior and to the role which locus of control may have in shaping coping strategies.

Additionally, this chapter has focused on some of the broader level obstacles faced by black women as entrepreneurs. While any entrepreneur is by definition faced with a variety of problems or stressors, the black woman entrepreneur faces additional pressures as a result of her gender and ethnicity. The cultural and historical materials discussed in this chapter are important in that they provide the context within which more theoretical concepts can be applied.

This literature review has defined the variables used in the study and provides the necessary background to construct a conceptual framework providing guidance for the data analysis, hypothesis testing, and interpretation of the results. The framework, presented in the following chapter, details the relationship among locus of control, stressors, dimensions of the coping process, and coping behaviors.

III

Conceptual Framework

This study examines the affect that locus of control beliefs of black women entrepreneurs have on their coping with business problems and the resultant level of business success. A cognitive stress and coping paradigm is used as the theoretical framework for testing the relative influence of locus of control beliefs versus situational factors on the selection of coping behaviors and coping outcomes. Business problems are viewed as stressors and as generating coping behaviors.

This chapter includes the components and the dynamics of the coping process. Following the discussion of the various levels of coping, a model of the stressor-appraisal-coping paradigm adapted for testing the hypotheses of this study is presented. This model considers relationships among business problems, one specific appraisal factor, coping behaviors, and outcomes of black women entrepreneurs (see Figure 3).

In contrast to Chapter Two and Figure 1 which discussed and provided a pictorial representation of all the facets of coping, this conceptual chapter will delineate only those aspects of the theory that will be the focus of this study.

Figure 2	Stressor-Appraisal-Coping Paradigm of Black Women Entrepreneurs	
	Examples of major Stressors: Money problems Lack of management skills Inadequate sales / customers	
<u>Personal Factors</u> Locus of control ↓	↓ Primary Appraisal ←——————→	<u>Environmental Factors</u> Family/sex/race
EXTERNALS-		INTERNALS+
↓ Emotion focused:	↓ Secondary Appraisal ←——————→	↓ Problem focused:
	↓ Coping Behaviors	
<u>Ineffective</u> Confrontive Distancing Escape avoidance	←——————→	<u>Effective</u> Accepting responsibility Planful problem solving self control social support
Less successful-	↓ Coping Outcomes ←——————→ Number of business problems Degree of business satisfaction Number of positive resolutions	More successful+

STRESSOR-APPRAISAL-COPING PARADIGM

Business Stressors

Black women face many obstacles as they attempt to become successful entrepreneurs. Chapter 2 discussed the broad range of problems that might be encountered by black women who own their own businesses: difficulties in finding capital, lack of relevant management experience, lack of customers or sales, and discrimination. This chapter focuses on the problems which have been particularly troublesome to black businesswomen business Over the years (Dingle, 1985; Thompson, 1988; Wall Street Journal, 2/28/85).

Money matters serve as the origin of many of the stressors of black business women. The first major stressor is to acquire sufficient capital to start the business. Obtaining initial capital to start a business is a factor for all entrepreneurs, however, accumulating money to finance a business is more difficult for black entrepreneurs. Black women have found that obtaining financial backing for their business is a major hurdle as women are seldom taken seriously in financial matters and their competence to operate a business ia seldom believed even when there is a proven record of success (Dingle, 1985; House Report 100-736; Wall Street Journal 2/12/93). According to the Los Angeles Times (June 30,1985) blacks received only nine and a half percent of the loans from the Small Business Administration in 1982.

Black women have special problems getting credit. Most financial institutions have been and continue to be reluctant to make loans to black women. To a certain extent, many officers of these institutions have difficulty accepting them as authentic, competent business persons. These views seem to be a combination of sexism and discrimination which involves the lack of acceptance of the black woman as an owner and leader in the enterprise regardless of her capabilities (Burlew, 1982; Griffin, 1986; Thompson, 1988).

Entrepreneurs constantly face high numbers of stressors. This may take the form of problems in meeting the weekly payroll, dealing with creditors, negotiating contracts, and customer relations. The black female who becomes an entrepreneur is immediately faced with the necessity of learning to cope with these stressors in such a way that the business can succeed and she can remain healthy (Boyd & Gumpert, 1983; Pelletier, 1982).

Appraisals

By definition, coping begins as the reaction to an event (Fleishman, 1984). However, it is not a reaction to the event itself, but rather to the individual's perception of that event. In order for persons to make satisfactory adaptations, they must be able to distinguish between benign and harmful stimuli or events (Lazarus, 1982). The appraisal process is central to coping and is heavily influenced by individuals' beliefs, values, and Commitments. Primary appraisal allows the individual to distinguish between irrelevant, beneficial, and harmful events. For example, if the primary appraisal determines the event is irrelevant to the individual, no more mental energy will be expended. However, if the event has some potential meaning to the individual's welfare, the preliminary appraisal is a primary factor in determining if it is potentially harmful or challenging (Lazarus, Averill & Opton, 1974).

Events appraised as being potentially harmful or threatening receive a secondary appraisal, in which alternatives for managing the event and resources available are weighed and balanced. An individual will make several different appraisals of events. Secondary appraisals represent an opportunity for individuals to undertake active problem solving or to reappraise the event as not being threatening. These re-appraisals may lead individuals to change the meanings attributed to the event (Lazarus & Folkman, 1984). Situations which are perceived as changeable often lead to positive reappraisals and renewed coping efforts (e.g. new problem solving efforts). Time required for appraisals of an event may vary from a few seconds to ongoing reappraisals over months or even years (Lazarus & Folkman, 1984).

Commitment is one of the most important factors among a number of elements that affect how events are appraised. Commitment is crucial in providing individual motivation, meaning and purpose to the coping effort. A certain level of commitment is necessary before the coping effort can be sustained. If commitment falters, the individual is vulnerable to inadequate or inconsistent coping behaviors (Lazarus & Folkman, 1984).

Beliefs also play a key role in the appraisal and coping process. Beliefs such as the need to achieve and religious convictions have been found to be quite an affect on how individuals appraise events (Lazarus & Folkman, 1984).

The values that individuals have determine what they find threatening. Examples include values learned in the family of origin, religious beliefs, and cultural identifications. The values and personal dispositions interact to produce both rational and irrational appraisals. Black women who have experienced previous detrimental events may have greater doubts regarding their ability to master new situations, as well as perceiving new situations as more threatening than they really are (Lazarus & Opton, 1966). Entrepreneurs who have much to lose or who think that a favorable outcome will be difficult to obtain, may be overwhelmed by strong emotions. These emotional reactions can interfere with rational problem solving efforts and lead to primitive, rigid, and ineffective coping behaviors. These variables shape and shade the meanings given to events and have a role in determining the nature of appraisals (Lazarus & Folkman, 1984).

Personal experiences are another element of the equation. The early childhood experiences of black women entrepreneurs in their family of origin are important influences on the views that influence their appraisals. In part early socialization against taking risks or staying with the security of working for others may serve to discourage entrepreneurship among professional African-American women, inspite of evidence of the probability of such ventures (Sullivan & McCracken, 1988). At the aggregate level, this may be related to socioeconomic status. The role models provided by parents, as well as the level of ongoing family and social support, are certainly important.

Epstein (1973) found that black professional women often came from families that emphasized the following values: personal achievement, the woman as a provider, thrift, and education. These findings are consistent with the views of Chestang (1977) in his study on achievement versus survival. He found that individuals who came from lower class families must discard survival attitudes in order to achieve personal success.

Whether or not people have been able to adequately handle stressors in the past will influence how they approach similar threats today. For example, persons who have developed significant coping skills and experienced many favorable outcomes in the past will have a strong sense of personal efficacy. They may be quite self-confident in their ability to cope with whatever challenges arise (Baumgardner, Heppner, & Arkin, 1986; Fleishman, 1984; Lazarus and Folkman,

1984). In contrast, individuals who have had negative experiences are likely to feel less competent to deal with the stressor (Barbarin, 1983; Lazarus & Folkman, 1984). With reference to black women, experiences of discrimination, oppression, and deprivation are additional influences helping to shape their appraisals of events (Gurin, Gurin, Lao, & Beattre, 1973).

Locus of Control

Human beings have always sought to find ways to control their fate. Beliefs in the gods, fate, and omens--and attempts to appeal to those powers to influence events--have been common in cultures throughout recorded history (Bromberg, 1975). One of the important factors shaping both the appraisals and ways of coping are individuals' beliefs about their ability to control their lives. Individuals who believe that what happens to them depends on what they do will appraise an event quite differently than individuals who believe that what happens to them is determined by chance, luck, fate, or powerful others.

Locus of control is a psychological construct referring to individual's beliefs about their ability to control what happens in their lives. When a person believes that events are the result of chance, luck, or fate, that individual is said to believe in external control. When an individual perceives that events are contingent on their own behavior (i.e. that their own actions can affect the outcome), they are said to have an internal locus of control (Rotter 1966). It is believed that persons with an internal locus of control are likely to appraise fewer events as threatening or stressful; thus, they are less distressed by potentially harmful events. The person with an internal locus of control will consider the way in which similar problems have been handled in the past, and are likely to regard the recurrence of those events as uneventful or challenging (Lefcourt, 1976; Anderson, 1977).

Persons with an external locus of control, however, may share certain characteristics with Type A individuals, who are highly anxious, always in a hurry, and easily threatened. These persons often have life experiences which leave them with lower self-confidence, impaired self-esteem and a sense of incompetence. As a result, many more events are likely to be appraised as threatening or stressful (Cohen, Kamarack, & Mermelstein, 1983; Nezer & Ronan, 1985; Kobasa, Maddi, & Courington, 1981).

Locus of control has been found to be related to entrepreneurship in at least three important ways: in the decision to become an entrepreneur, in the level of business activity, and in predicting success of the business operation (Borland, 1974; Panday & Tewary, 1979; Miller, 1983). Many small business owners belong to minority groups or are recent immigrants. In either case, it is believed that success is facilitated when the individual has an internal locus of control.

The locus of control variable has been operationalized in this study by the use of the Levenson Multi-dimensional Locus of Control Scale. Early research studies using the Rotter scale assumed that the concept being measured was unidimensional. However, as more and more researchers used the Rotter Scale, inconsistent and sometimes conflicting results began to be reported. Mirels (1970) and Abramowitz (1973) conducted studies to assess the unidimensionality of the I-E scale. Correlations between the I-E scores and other variables were often very low, and several problems with the scale were identified.

Mirels reported the results of factor analysis on data from a sample of 306 male and female undergraduate college students. Examination of the content of factors disclosed unclear differentiation between personal fate versus opinion regarding social institutions, as well as an inability to isolate beliefs characterized by faith in luck or chance as a factor determining a person's political or social effectiveness (Mirels, 1970).

Abramowitz (1973), as part of a larger project examining the psychological adjustment of student political activists, looked at the relationship between locus of control beliefs and socio-political activity. His results were also useful in assessing the assumed unidimensionality of the Rotter I-E Scale. Results were consistent with Mirels (1970), and strongly implied that the I-E Scale was actually measuring two quite different dimensions: non-political personal concerns and third person political reference material (Abramowitz, 1973).

There was clearly a need for an alternative and more sophisticated measure of locus of control. Levenson conducted several studies in the early 1970s designed to clarify the external dimension of I-E Scale. The work Mirels and Abramowitz suggested that there were two components of the external dimension: (a) belief in control of outcomes by luck, chance or fate, and (b) belief in control of outcomes by the political system or powerful others (Abramowitz, 1973). Levenson (1973) developed an instrument with three eight-item sub-scales measuring three types of control beliefs: belief in events as controlled by luck or chance (referred to as the "C" scale), belief in events as controlled by powerful others ("P" scale), a belief in a personal ability to control events ("I" scale). These scales were developed and validated in a study of social activism, with subjects consisting of psychiatric patients. The scales were found to be conceptually pure, with no overlap among the factors. Subsequent studies using samples of political activists, undergraduate students, and parents showed high levels of validity and reliability, implying that the scales were accurately measuring control beliefs (Levenson, 1973, 1974, 1975).

While numerous studies have explored the dynamics of locus of control beliefs, none have been done on black women entrepreneurs. Lefcourt and Ladwig (1965) in their study of 120 inmates of correctional institutions found consistent differences in the internal versus external orientations between black and white prisoners. They thought that the discrimination and segregation which blacks persons experience facilitates an external orientation. The findings of Lefcourt and Ladwig have been supported in studies by other researchers; however, Gurin, Gurin, Lao, and Beattre (1972) pointed out some of the benefits of being more externally oriented for black persons. The studies by Gurin and colleagues have found that black males and females differ on locus of control measures from whites, and that environmental experiences have an influence on shaping locus of control beliefs.

They found that the class and discrimination experiences of black youth resulted in a more complex and multilevel belief system regarding what controls ones' lives and success. While subscribing generally to societal values regarding the necessity of hard work for success, black persons were aware of the influence of discrimination and class limited opportunities on their potential for personal success. Gurin and associates observed that these views were found to be not only healthy but functional, for they lead to more realistic assessment of black persons chances for success and also led to less psychic damage that can result from excessive self-blaming tendencies that have been noted by other writers.

Before meaningful conclusions can be drawn on the relationship among locus of control beliefs of black women entrepreneurs, their handling of business stressors, and their achievement of business success, research must be done on samples of black women owning and operating their enterprises. Although the studies above point to the complexity of measuring the beliefs that black persons hold, predicting whether the subjects of these study will score similar to the black persons in the earlier studies is highly unlikely as the subjects of this study have many different characteristics. The studies are being done with more than twenty years difference in time. It is not known how many of the subjects in the previous studies were women. Undoubtedly, there are many class and life experience differences among the subjects as well.

Coping Behaviors

Following an appraisal of any event as representing a threat, individuals will initiate coping responses to manage the event. Coping behaviors take many forms, but two primary modes of coping responses, emotion-focused and problem-solving, may be distinguished (Lazarus, 1981). Individuals develop coping styles which are preferred for dealing with threatening events. Their coping responses consist of strategies based on skills, feelings of personal efficacy and self confidence, and modes of approaching situations accumulated over their lifetime. Individuals who have learned to utilize their knowledge and ability to solve problems in the past are likely to adopt a problem-solving coping style for dealing with problems of all types. Other persons may be more effective working with others, and may therefore develop a style characterized by communication and seeking social support. Previous negative experiences in the past also play a role, and such beliefs as "you can't fight city hall" or that problems represent judgments by God or fate will adversely affect the coping efforts of individuals (Lazarus & Folkman, 1984).

The coping process often involves the use of material and social resources. Material resources may include financial assets, lines of credit, or assets of others in managing stressful situations. Examples of social resources may include direct involvement of other persons based on friendships, political contacts, or business relationships. Family and kinship networks are important as coping resources as well.

The variables for coping responses were operationalized by the Ways of Coping questionnaire developed by Folkman and Larzarus (1984) as revised in 1986. Lazarus and colleagues developed a questionnaire to measure the ways individuals cope with stressful events. Their initial questionnaire measured coping as a dichotomous variable, i.e. problem focused (interpersonal) and emotion focused (intrapsychic) coping (Folkman and Lazarus, 1980). Subsequently, they identified eight dimensions of coping which are useful for understanding the complex relationship among coping appraisals, behaviors, and outcomes. These coping behaviors are confrontive, distancing, self-control, seeking social support, accepting responsibility, escape-avoidance, positive reappraisal and planful problem solving (Folkman & Lazarus, 1985, 1986).

Lazarus and colleagues (1984,1985, & 1986) discovered that coping behaviors are highly sensitive to situational variables. Typically, when threats concerning self-esteem are involved, coping behaviors such as self-control, accepting responsibility, confrontive coping, escape-avoidance, and seeking social support are likely to be used. In situations where a loss of respect for someone else is involved, confrontive coping and self-control are likely to be used. When the threatening event is related to work or finances, individuals are more likely to use self-control, planful problem solving, confrontive coping, and to seek social support. When the stakes are appraised as being very high, regardless of the nature of the problems, persons tend to exercise more self-control, escape avoidance, and to seek social support (Folkman, Lazarus, Dunkel-Schetter, Delongis, & Gruen, 1986).

Coping Outcomes

Stressful events are of varying length, and the evaluation of the outcome of particular coping behaviors is problematic due to dynamic and continuous relationship between individuals and their environment. In addressing the problem, Folkman and Lazarus (1984) categorized coping outcomes as either satisfactory or unsatisfactory based on self-reports. Events with satisfactory outcomes were frequently associated with changeable situations and unsatisfactory outcomes often occurred in situations perceived as unchangeable or involving a loss.

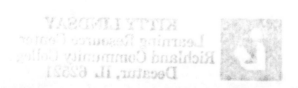

The result of coping efforts may depend on factors beyond the specific individual actions taken. For example, outcomes of stressful episodes are also a function of environmental and social constraints. In addition, social institutions may be so unresponsive that the impact of personal coping efforts are completely outweighed (Lazarus & Folkman, 1984; Pearlin & Schooler, 1978).

SUMMARY OF CONCEPTUAL FRAMEWORK

In summary, the conceptual model utilized in this study is shown schematically in Figure 2. Black women entrepreneurs, when encountering a new event, will make a primary appraisal of that event to determine whether it has meaning for their well-being. If the event is determined to represent a potential threat, harm, or challenge to their business survival or success a secondary appraisal is made to determine what actions should be taken and what resources they have psychologically, behaviorally, socially, and materially to manage the situation.

Both the appraisal of the situation and the specific coping behavior chosen are shaped by many factors. Of the most theoretical important are the nature of the beliefs that the entrepreneurs have regarding what controls their lives. Locus of control beliefs are thought to influence the appraisals and selections of coping behaviors of black women entrepreneurs. Additional influences that help to pattern coping styles are the environmental experiences related to family practices, socio-economic level, discrimination, and gender-related encounters. Locus of control beliefs are the only appraisal variables that have been operationalized in this study.

Coping behaviors are multi-dimensional. Much coping takes place on the physical level. Other coping efforts are intrapsychic, involving such efforts as thinking, planning, or palliative measures. Coping efforts are also behavioral involving action and interpersonal activities. The variables of coping behaviors are operationalized in this study by the Ways of Coping Questionnaire developed by Lazarus and Folkman at the University of California at Berkeley. Lazarus and colleagues found that coping measures were highly responsive to situational variables.

Coping by African-American women entrepreneurs can be expected to vary in accordance to the specific circumstances in which the business problem occurs and also to the level of threat to the business that the problem poses. The black women entrepreneurs who make up the sample for this study are drawn largely from California, live in urban areas and are highly educated. We can speculate that they are especially interested in and knowledgeable about how society works and how to cope with their environment. We know   that they have been very successful in dealing with the educational institutions. We can expect that these women have developed a certain amount of personal efficacy and that they have established patterns of behaviors to manage stressors in their environment and businesses.

The factors considered in this chapter will serve as guides to collect and test the data. The hypotheses for the study, the methods of the data collection, and specifics for testing are presented in the following chapter.

IV

Methodology

This chapter provides a description of the general purpose of the study and the research design to be employed. The specific objectives are stated and methodological issues are addressed. These include: the description of the sample, study variables, definition of terms, instrumentation, data collection, data analysis procedures, and limitations and assumptions of the study.

PURPOSE OF THE STUDY

There has been little empirical research focusing on black business women and as a result there exist many gaps in our knowledge about them and the problems they face. Little is known about the demographic characteristics of this population. Information on the major problems black women encounter in their businesses, as well as how they cope with those problems, is also unavailable.

The purpose of this research is to address this gap in the literature by studying a sample of black women entrepreneurs. The focus of the project is to assess the effects of demographic characteristics and attitudes about locus of control on coping behaviors.

Specific research issues addressed in the analysis included the following areas:

1. The nature of their beliefs regarding locus of control;
2. The relationship of those beliefs to the success of their business operations;

3. The relationship of those beliefs to the level of satisfaction they derive from their business;

4. The relationship of those beliefs to the types of coping behaviors they use in dealing with their business problems.

With regard to coping behaviors, more specific research questions included: How much of the variance in coping behavior can be explained by variation in control beliefs? What other variables have a significant effect in shaping coping behaviors? How do coping behaviors vary given the degree of business risk in differing business situations? The literature suggests that at a certain high level of risk particular coping patterns may emerge which outweigh individual locus of control characteristics. This issue was also addressed in the data analysis.

THEOREMS

The general theorem of the study is that variations in the control beliefs of black women entrepreneurs will account for most of the variance in their selection of coping behaviors. This implies that entrepreneurs characterized by an internal locus of control will differ significantly in their choice of coping behaviors from entrepreneurs characterized by either Powerful Others or Chance locus of control. In order to determine if African-American women entrepreneurs have similar characteristics and deal with their business stressors in ways found to exist among entrepreneurs generally, the theorems of this study had to be operationalized by testable propositions. Each of the major theorems was restated as specific testable suppositions and tested at the $p = .05$ level of significance.

Theorem I was that subjects with an external locus of control will utilize confronting, distancing, and escape avoidance as coping behaviors to a greater extent than subjects with an internal locus of control.

Studies by Anderson (1973), Pendary & Tewary (1979) on entrepreneurs found that entrepreneurs with an internal locus of control were more active and effective in their business activities. The studies of Folkman and Lazarus using middle class and middle age subjects (1980, 1984, and 1986) found that certain coping behaviors were more effective. Therefore, it is predicted that black women entrepreneurs who have an internal locus of control will be characterized by an internal locus of control and will utilize more effective coping behaviors.

Studies by Myers (1980) and Lykes, (1983) that found black women to be better copers, cited some of the behaviors that the women used. These studies showed that whether the women took direct action or used indirect methods, the means they used were effective.

Since Lazarus and Folkman studies of coping behaviors took place over several years and interviewed subjects a number of times, they were able to determine the effectiveness of certain behaviors. The behaviors listed in this research question were ineffective in bringing about the desired results. Subjects in this study that rely on these behaviors to solve business problems are predicted to score higher on the sub-scales for external locus of control.

Theorem I was restated as three testable sub-theorems with external locus of control serving as the independent variable and each type of ineffective coping behavior stated as the dependent variable. A prediction of the selection of the coping behaviors was made for the subjects in accordance with their control beliefs as evidenced by their scores on the Levenson Scales. For example, each the sub-theorems was stated as subjects with an external locus of control will utilize confrontative coping behavior to a greater extent than persons with an internal locus. The next sub-theorem was stated as subjects with an external locus of control will utilize distancing coping behavior to a greater extent than subjects with an internal locus of control, etc.

Theorem II was that subjects with an internal locus of control will utilize self control, social support, accepting responsibility, positive reappraisal and planful problem solving to a greater extent than persons with external locus of control.

The literature, both fiction and nonfiction, contains many accounts of black women who have been active and creative in surmounting the environmental conditions to acquire economic self-sufficiency (Giddings, 1984; Ledsock, 1984; Lykes, 1983). The behaviors listed in the above supposition are felt to be those characteristic of responsible successful individuals. The literature on entrepreneurs have demonstrated that business owners who are more active and planful in their activities have higher rates of business success. These entrepreneurs have also been found to be characterized by an internal locus of control.

Subira (1986) and Johnson (1985) in studies of black business owners noted that entrepreneurs that follow sound business practices and behaviors that are typical of the behaviors above are more effective in their business endeavors. Although their studies did not differentiate between men and women, there is no reason to think that effective behaviors would differ by sex. It is predicted that the black women entrepreneurs, who score higher on the internal locus of control scales, will cope in a manner consistent with successful black male entrepreneurs. This prediction is reasonable given that a number of empirical researchers on coping have found that there is no significant gender related differences in coping behaviors.

Theorem II was restated in the same manner as Theorem I as five testable sub-theorems with internal locus of control serving as the independent variable. Each coping behavior considered as an effective coping action was stated as the dependent variable in one of the five tests. For example, subjects with internal locus of control would utilize self-control coping behaviors to a greater extent than participants with an external locus of control.

Theorem III was restated as subjects with serious business problems will utilize self-control, escape avoidance and seeking social support to a greater degree than subjects with less serious problems, regardless of the type of locus of control.

Folkman and Lazarus (1986) determined that the selection of coping behaviors were closely tied to situational variables. They found that when the stakes were high that most persons tended to select specific coping strategies. We can expect that the black women entrepreneurs will be typical of other persons who are functioning in the American business community.

These subjects are living during times when there is some choice whether to work for someone else or to be self employed. The decision to work for themselves is expected to be based on the beliefs that they can handle their own economic lives. Serious threats to the business can be expected to be a stressful event for the entrepreneur as such an occurrence would bring into question their decision to quit a job with a high salary, substantial benefits, and good job security.

Most new business owners use their own savings to start their businesses. This fact is true for the majority of African-American women entrepreneurs. Also, family members may have invested in or be working in the business. These factors mean that whenever the subjects are faced with a serious business problem, they can be expected to behave like other persons with problems where the stakes are high. Lost of the business would mean severe damage in many areas of their lives, such as their career, financial, and relationships to family and friends.

Theorem III was restated as three testable sub-theorems as follows: a) subjects with serious business problems will utilize self-control as a coping behavior to a greater degree than subjects without a serious business problem, b) subjects with a serious business problem will utilize the coping behavior of escape avoidance to a greater degree than those subjects without a serious business problem, and c) subjects with a serious business problem will seek social support as a coping behavior to a greater extent than those persons without a serious business problem.

In addition, three theorems regarding internal versus external locus of control beliefs in relationship to other characteristics of the entrepreneurs in the sample were evaluated by operationalizing each of the propositions. A prototype of these testable theorems is stated as subjects with an internal locus of control will have fewer business problems than subjects with an external locus of control.

Black women entrepreneurs can be expected to have many of the characteristics of male entrepreneurs, including similarity in locus of control beliefs. Further it is thought that similar beliefs and functioning should produce similar results.

African-American women have not been found to have the fear of success that is often typical of white women (Fleming, 1982; Gilkes, 1982; Gump, 1975; Puryear & Mednick, 1974). It is often thought that these differences are related to the less favorable position in society of black women as compare to white women and the higher rates of participation in the labor force (Smith & Stewart, 1983). These differences could also be related to familial expectations that the black woman will provide for herself and her family in spite of marriage and the birth of children (Epstein, 1973).

Whereas many African-American women have been found to be highly religious. Such women are said to believe what happens is God's will and a matter of fate. It's questionable whether being religious will affect their beliefs about locus of control. Therefore, it is predicted that black women who score high on the internal locus of control scales will developed better coping strategies, which will produce fewer business stressors, better coping outcomes and greater satisfaction with their businesses.

STUDY VARIABLES

The primary outcomes of interest are coping behaviors, as measured by Lazarus and Folkman's (1986) Ways of Coping Scale. These coping behaviors are the dependent variables in the study. The behaviors generates eight distinct sub-scales: confronting, distancing, self-control, seeking social support, accepting responsibility, escape avoidance, planful problem solving, and positive reappraisal. Each of these coping actions will be assessed with regard to potentially threatening business situations which the subjects have encountered.

The primary independent variable is the locus of control, as measured by the Levenson Multi-dimensional Locus of Control Scale. The three basic types of locus of control are Internal (I), Powerful Others (P), and Chance (C) .

Other covariates taken into account included the level of risk to the business posed by the specific problem, and the level of satisfaction on the part of the subject.

Definition of Terms

Business Problems: Business problems were categorized money, customer relations, sales, equipment, labor (personnel), and business organizations. Subjects were asked to check specific problems in each category which they had encountered at anytime since they had been in business.

Business satisfaction: Subject responses to statements of financial rewards, personal rewards and feelings were assigned + 1 for positive responses and -1 for negative responses. These values were then summed to provide an overall measure of business satisfaction, as well as sub-scales for financial rewards, personal rewards, and feelings.

Confrontative coping behaviors: These are measured by responses to statements such as: I stood my ground and fought for what I wanted; tried to get the person responsible to change his or her mind; I expressed anger to the person(s) who caused the problem.

Distancing: Subjects were asked to what extent they engaged in behaviors such as 1) made light of the situation; refused to get too serious about it; 2) went on as if nothing had happened; 3) didn't let it get to me; refused to think about it too much.

Escape avoidance: Subjects were asked to what extent they engaged in behaviors such as: 1) wished the situation would go away or somehow be over; 2) hoped a miracle would happen; 3) made myself better by eating, drinking, using drugs, etc.

External Locus of Control: Subjects who score high on either the Powerful Others or Chance sub-scale.

Internal Locus of Control: Subjects who score high on the Internal Locus of Control sub-scale.

Lager business size: More employees and higher gross receipts.

Planful problem-solving: Statements used to measure this coping behavior are 1) I knew what had to be done, so I doubled my efforts to make things work. 2) I made a plan of action and followed it.

Positive reappraisal: Sample statements used to evaluate this behavior are 1) changed or grew as a person; 2) I came out of the experience better than when I went in; 3) found new faith.

Positive Resolutions of Business Problems: Subjects were asked to evaluate their own level of satisfaction with regard to the resolution of the problem and the effect of the resolution of the problem on the business.

Seeking social support: This hypothesis was tested by evaluating the subjects' responses to such statements as:
1) talked to someone to find out more about the situation; 2) talked to someone who could do something concrete about the problem.
Accepting responsibility: Examples of Statements used to evaluate the coping behaviors in this area were 1) criticized or lectured myself or 2) realized I had brought the problem on myself.

Self-control: Subjects were asked to state their use of such behaviors such statements as 1) I tried to keep my feelings to myself; 2) kept others from knowing how bad things were; 3) tried not to burn my bridges, but leave things open somewhat.

Serious business problem: Business problems assessed as 6 or greater on a scale from 1 to 10 were defined as being serious business problems.

Stressor: Any business problem which must be managed by the entrepreneur.

STUDY SAMPLE

The names and addresses of black women entrepreneurs were obtained from business directories, registries of business owners who qualified as disadvantaged or minority contracts with public agencies, membership lists of business organizations and personal referrals. Approximately 525 questionnaires were mailed; 105 questionnaires were returned, for an overall response rate of 20.0%. Of the returned questionnaires, 21 were eliminated due to incomplete data, late return, or because they were completed by males. Thus, the final sample consisted of 84 black women entrepreneurs. The response rate of 20% is acceptable, and, the sample size provides a sufficient statistical base for testing the stated hypotheses. However, the sample is limited in its' ability to render predictionable results as representative of black women entrepreneurs across the United States.

Instrumentation

Levenson Multi-dimensional Locus of Control Scale. This scale consists of 24 items which are scored using a Likert format, yielding the three sub-scales of eight items each. These are Internal Control, Powerful Others Control, and Chance Control each of which may range from 0-48.

Levenson developed her instrument in order to improve on the Rotter (1966) Internal - External (IE) Scale. Levenson (1974) and Mirels (1970) both found that the factors in the I-E Scale were related more to individual beliefs regarding their ability to control their own lives than to their ability to influence the social system. The I-E Scale also failed to deal with chance as a source of control, and Levenson attempted to address this by operationalizing three sources of control internal control (I), chance control (C), and powerful others control (P).

Levenson evaluated the construct validity of the scales in several different research settings. In two additional studies the three scales had almost no overlap and most statements loading greater than 0.50 (Levenson, 1974). A further study resulted in highly significant correlations with Mirel's scale of social system control (Levenson, 1974).

Reliability characteristics of the scales were found to be only moderately high, which may be attributed to the variety of situations in which the scales were tested (Levenson, 1974). Reported reliability coefficients are shown in Table 3. These coefficients compare favorably with those obtained by Rotter and are in the range generally considered as acceptable.

Table 2
Reliability Coefficients for Levenson Scales

Kuber-Subscale	Split Richardson		Test-half	Retest
Powerful Others	.77	.66	.74	
Chance	.78	.64	.78	
Internal	.64	.62	.64	

Ways of Coping Questionnaire

This scale was developed by Dr. Susan Folkman and Dr. Richard Lazarus at the University of California at Berkeley. This measure differed from previous measures in that it was dynamic and focused on what actions subjects would actually make during a specific event. The initial questionnaire consisted of a checklist of 68 items with forced binary answers (Folkman & Lazarus, 1980). The list was revised into a 66 item self report measure utilizing a four-point Likert scale format. This permitted the use of analysis of variance and factor analysis. Eight sub-scales were subsequently developed after clarification, rewording, and elimination of unclear items.

The final revision of the Ways of Coping Questionnaire was designed to address the relationship of appraisal to coping and coping to outcomes. Each coping behavior is measured by six or seven specific activities. The subjects indicate their behavior by circling O to 3 opposite the statement on the questionnaire. A four-point Likert Scale (O=not used, 1=used somewhat, 2=used quite a bit, and 3=used a great deal) measures the extent of the coping behavior's use. Sample statements for each way of coping are; Self-control - I tried not to act too hastily or follow my first hunch; Escape Avoidance - refused to believe it had happened; and Seeking Social Support - accepted sympathy and understanding from someone (see appendix A for a complete copy of the sub-scales).

Validity of the scales was assessed using factor analysis with oblique rotation. Intercorrelations of the items were examined and used in forming the scales. The final scales contained seven distinct scales: confrontative coping, distancing, self controlling, seeking social support, accepting responsibility, escape-avoidance, and positive reappraisal. These scales were found to have a high degree of construct validity, and to account for 46.2% of the variance in coping behaviors (Folkman & Lazarus, 1986). Intercorrelations are shown in Table 3.

Table 3
Coping Scales Intercorrelation

Scale	1	2	3	4	5	6	7	8
Confrontative Coping		.01	.36	.27	.26	.27	.28	.26
Distancing			.36	-.04	.27	.32	.09	.26
Self Controlling				.24	.30	.36	.57	.39
Seeking Social Support					.09	.23	.30	.32
Accepting Responsibility						.39	.13	.18
Escape Avoidance							.10	.23
Planful Problem Solving								.39
Positive Reappraisal								1.00

In order to assess the internal consistency of each scale, Cronbach's alpha coefficients were computed. These are shown in Table 4. Alpha coefficients range from .61 for distancing to .79 for positive reappraisal, with all values being in the acceptable range.

Table 4
Reliability Coefficients for Ways of Coping Scales

Confrontive Coping	.70
Distancing	.61
Self Controlling	.70
Seeking Social Support	.76
Accepting Responsibility	.66
Escape Avoidance	.72
Positive Reappraisal	.79
Planful Problem Solving	.73

Background Questionnaire

This instrument, developed for the study, included sections assessing socioeconomic and family background, customer profiles, business support, and specific business 94 problems. In the final section, subjects were asked to identify one specific problem and to indicate how they dealt with it, whether the outcome was satisfactory and to assess the impact of the results on the business.

Most questions were multiple response. A pretest indicated that the questions were understandable and that the form could be completed in 30-40 minutes. Copies of the background questionnaire and the instruments are included in Appendix A.

Procedures

Subjects were mailed a questionnaire to collect the data collection. Each packet included a cover letter explaining the project, a consent form, the instruments, and a self-addressed stamped envelope to facilitate timely return of the data. The telephone numbers of the project director, the chairperson of the planning committee and the Institutional Review Board were included in the cover letter.

Data Analysis

Initial data analysis provided a profile of the sample, utilizing descriptive statistics and frequency distributions. Correlations of all internal level variables were computed, and cross-tabulations of categorical variables were done. The Chi-square statistic was used to evaluate statistical significance.

The theorems were evaluated at the $p = .05$ significance level. Theorems I and II explicitly compared two groups (internal versus external locus of control) on the scores on each of the sub-scales of the Ways of Coping Scale. The appropriate technique was the t-test. Theorem III implied that the locus of control be controlled for, since two independent variables (serious versus non-serious problems and internal versus external locus of control) are specified in each comparison. Thus, analysis of variance was used to test theorem III. However, due to the lack of significance for two of the three ways of coping, the two-way Anova tests was dropped in favor of a series of t-tests for each sub-theorem. Theorem IV through VIII are straightforward comparisons of the two groups, and again utilized the t-test statistic.

Exploratory analysis was also done. Regression analysis with specific types of coping behavior as dependent variables (e.g. positive reappraisal) were done to identify independent variables predictive of effective coping behaviors in this population. None of the independent variables (e.g. age, marital status, education) were found to account for significant variation in coping behavior.

Results of the theorem tests and data analyses are reported in the next chapter, with the exception of the regression analysis which was non-productive.

V

Results

This chapter presents the results of the study. This includes a discussion of the characteristics of the sample, their businesses, and the results of the theorem tests.

PROFILE OF STUDY SAMPLE

All of the subjects were born in the United States, but only 27.4 percent were native Californians. Five respondents were born in the San Francisco Bay Area, with another 18 born elsewhere in California. The largest proportion of respondents (28.6%) were born in the Southern states. Table 5 shows the distribution of place of birth of the subjects.

Table 5
Place of Birth of Subjects

Region	Number	Percent
Bay Area	5	6.0%
Other California areas	18	21.4%
Southwest	1	1.2%
South	24	28.6%
Atlantic & Northeast	19	22.6%
Midwest	16	19.0%
Northwest	1	1.2%

Subjects ranged in age from 27 to 70 years, with a mean age of 41.78 years. The majority of the subjects were in their 40's, and more than 90 percent were under 50 years Old.

Marital status of subjects is shown in Table 6. The majority of the subjects were either single or divorce/separated with only 36.9 percent of the subjects currently married.

Table 6
Marital Status of Subjects

Status	Number	Percent
Single	18	21.4%
Married	31	36.9%
Divorced/Separated	27	32.1%
Widowed	8	9.5%

As shown in Table 7 there were few children among the sample, with a third of the entrepreneurs having no children, and an additional 23 percent having one child. The subjects with young children are all currently married. The mean number of children was 1.46; however, 13 subjects accounted for 60 percent of the children.

Table 7
Children of the Entrepreneurs

Children	Number	Percent
0	27	32.14%
1	19	22.62%
2	23	27.38%
3	8	9.52%
4	5	5.95%

In general, subjects were highly educated, with most (89.2%) having attended college. Almost 75 percent of the sample had a college degree, with slightly over half having earned graduate degrees. Table 8 shows the level of education of the subjects.

Table 8
Educational Level of Subjects

Education	Number	Percent
High School Grad or Less	1	1.2%
Technical/Specialized	8	9.6%
Some College	12	14.5%
College Degree	20	24.1%
Grad Degree	42	50.6%

Most subjects had been employed prior to starting their own business, and virtually all of the previously employed subjects had held white collar jobs. As shown in Table 9, more than 64 percent of the sample had held professional or administrative positions. Only 13 percent of the women had been unemployed, housewives, or retired.

Table 9
Prior Occupation of Subjects

Occupation	Number	Percent
Executive/Professional	9	11.8%
Managerial	2	2.6%
Administrative	38	50.0%
Clerical	15	19.7%
Skilled Manual	2	2.6%
Unemployed/Housewives	8	10.5%
Retired	2	2.6%

The size of the family of origin was highly variable. Four of the subjects were only children, with the largest family of origin having seventeen children. The mean number of siblings was 3.94. Subjects tended to be the older children in the family. Thirty-two percent of the women were the first born; with nineteen percent being the second oldest.

Although 75.1 percent of subjects' fathers were blue collar workers and 73.7 percent had only a high school education or less, 44.3 percent of the fathers had owned their own businesses or were self-employed. Subjects' mothers were housewives (33.3%), had white collar jobs (17.9% clerical, 25.6 administrative or minor professionals), or owned their own business (24.6%).

The data indicated that the subjects' families played an important role in their business in key areas. They served as a source of capital for business. Notably, 16.5 percent of the subjects indicated that loans from relatives had provided the initial financing for their business ventures. Family members were employed in 39.3 percent of the businesses, with the largest number of relatives working in the business being seven.

In addition, family members and relatives represented a major source of social support for the entrepreneur. Family members were listed as the most important source of moral support by 59.3 percent of the sample. Table 10, following, provides a profile of the most important sources of social support.

Table 10
Sources of Social Support

Source of Support	Number	Percent
Spouse/Children	34	42.0%
Parents/Siblings	14	17.3%
Close Friends	14	17.3%
Self	10	12.3%
Professional Organizations or Colleagues	4	4.9%
Partners	2	2.5%
Spiritual	2	2.5%
Customers	1	1.2%

PROFILE OF THE BUSINESSES

Location
Over 85 percent of the subjects operate businesses located in California. Twenty-nine businesses (33.7%) were in the Bay Area, with 45 businesses (52.3%) located elsewhere in California. The other businesses were scattered around the country (i.e. Southwest, South, and Northeast regions).

Type of Business
These businesses are typical of those operated by small business entrepreneurs. Over 70 percent of the businesses were classified as services such as professional, personal, and technical. Examples of professional services included medical, legal, financial, management consultation, and psychotherapy. Technical services businesses included medical and educational research, computer program development, and laboratory services. Personal services included beauty salons, day-care centers, rest homes, physical fitness centers, and health clubs. The subjects operated 17 percent of businesses in manufacturing, construction, wholesale and retail trade, security services, trucking and transportation, and product distribution.

Most of the businesses were started in the last ten years (75.3% since 1980 and 30.6% since 1985). For 65.9 percent of the subjects, this was their first business. About a fifth (22.4%) had interests in other businesses, but only one subject had business operations in more than one state.

Sources of Funding

The majority of the entrepreneurs (62.4%) were sole proprietors. Another 25.9 percent operate closed corporations, and 10.6 percent have businesses with partnerships. One of the subjects reported operating a publicly held corporation. The majority of the subjects (82.1%) financed their businesses out of personal assets and savings, although some had obtained additional capital through loans from family members and friends. Others were able to secure initial capital from investors or loans from banks. A few entrepreneurs had multiple sources of start-up funding.

Size of Business

Most of the businesses operated by the subjects were quite small, with fifty percent having 3 employees, or less, and 75 percent of the businesses having 6 employees or less. Fewer than 10 percent of the businesses had 35 employees or more, although the largest business had 98 employees. The gross receipts of the businesses show the same skewed distribution. While the mean gross income was $299,484.00, the standard deviation was $563,829. Fifty percent of the businesses had income of $79,000 or less, and 75 percent of the businesses earned $250,000 per year or less.

Scope of Business

The subjects operated predominately local enterprises, with 38.6 percent of the businesses serving their own city and another 24.1 percent serving neighboring towns and counties. Several of the subjects operated statewide (7.2%), and a few small import-export firms (8.4%) had an international market. Some of the larger firms (21.7%) had customers nationwide. The businesses served mixed ethnic markets (24.7% whites, 25.9% minorities, and 49.4% the general public).

Business Problems

Subjects were asked to check problems they had encountered from a list of twenty problems. A number of the entrepreneurs felt that they had not encountered any problem of significance. Not surprisingly, money problems were the most frequently encountered (i.e. cash flow, difficulty in getting financing and credit to start and expand their businesses). The entrepreneurs frequently did not know how to identify new customers or to make effective use of advertisement. Personnel problems were another source of trouble. Subjects were either unable to find skilled labor or to afford the salaries demanded by skilled laborers, and some firms were bothered by a significant amount of staff conflict. Table 11 below presents the problems identified.

Table 11
Reported Problems

Type of Problem	Number	Percent
Cash Flow	19	21.1
Business Skills (i.e. marketing, inventory)	17	21.5
Personnel	12	15.2
Credit/Financing	9	11.5
Suppliers	9	11.5
Time Management	5	6.3
Legal/Bureaucratic	5	6.3
Partners	5	6.3
Discrimination	3	3.8

PRELIMINARY ANALYSIS OF CORRELATIONS

Correlations among the Levenson Sub-scales are shown in Table 12. As expected, the correlation between the Powerful Other (P) and Chance (C) sub-scales was positive and highly significant.

The correlation of Internal Locus of Control (I) with both P and C sub-scales was negative and significant.

Table 12
Intercorrelations of Locus of Control sub-scales

	Powerful Other	Chance	Internal
Powerful Other	1.00	0.74***	-0.25**
Chance		1.00	-0.22*
Internal			1.00

*p< = .05; **p< = .01; ***p< = .001

Due to the high degree of correlation between the P and C Sub-scales (p< = .001), it was not possible to clearly distinguish subjects as having one or the other type of external control. Instead, subjects who scored above the median on the Internal sub-scale and below the median on the Powerful Other and Chance scales were defined as having an Internal Locus of Control. Remaining subjects were classified as having an External Locus of Control. These locus of control groups, based on scores on the Levenson Multi-dimensional Locus of Control Scale, are utilized in the hypothesis tests which follow.

Theorem Tests

The first theorem referred to the relationship between locus of control and confronting, distancing, and escape avoidance as coping behaviors. The three specific theorems to be tested are: a) Subjects with an external locus of control will utilize confrontative coping behavior to a greater extent than persons with an internal locus of control, b) Persons with an external locus of control will utilize distancing as a coping behavior to a greater extent than persons with an internal locus of control, and c) Subjects with external locus of control will utilize coping behaviors of escape avoidance to a greater extent than persons with an internal locus of control.

The t-test was used to test the differences between the two groups for each of the three sub-theorems. The criterion used for evaluation was the $p = .05$ level of significance. There were no significant differences between the two groups on any of the coping sub-scales. In fact, as shown in Table 13, there is a trend in the opposite direction than expected. Thus, the findings do not support theorems IA, IB, or IC.

Table 13
Theorem #1

Way of Coping	GROUP		
	Internal Locus of Control(n = 39)	External Locus of Control(n = 41)	t-test
Confrontive	6.56	5.73	-1.14
Distancing	5.62	4.83	-0.93
Escape-Avoidance	5.46	4.15	-1.41

The second theorem referred to the relationship between locus of control and self-control, social support, accepting responsibility, positive re-appraisal, and planful problem solving. This led to the formulation of the following five specific theorems: a) Participants with internal locus of control will utilize self-control coping behaviors to a greater extent than participants with an external locus of control, b) Participants with an internal locus of control will utilize seeking social support to a greater extent than subjects with an external locus of control, c) Participants with internal locus of control will utilize coping behavior of accepting responsibility to a greater extent than participants with an external locus of control, d) Participants with an internal locus of control will utilize positive reappraisal to a greater extent than participants with an external locus of control, and e) Participants with an internal locus of control will use planful problem solving to a greater extent than participants with an external locus of control.

Each of these sub-theorems was tested using the t-test to evaluate the differences between the two groups, with the .05 level of significance at the criterion. Again, as shown in Table 14, there were no significant difference between the two groups in any of the five coping sub-scales. Therefore, there was no support for Theorem II.

Table 14
Theorem #2

Way of Coping	Internal Locus of Control($n=39$)	External Locus of Control($n=41$)	t-test
Self-Controlling	9.98	9.78	-0.19
Seeking Social Support	8.38	8.51	0.13
Accepting Responsibility	4.56	3.88	-1.17
Positive Reappraisal	11.02	11.44	0.36
Planful Problem Solving	9.43	10.64	1.35

*p < = .05; **p < = .01

The third theorem referred to the relationship between the seriousness of business problems and the coping behaviors of self-control, escape avoidance and seeking social support. This led to three testable theorems: a) Participants with serious business problems will utilize self-control as a coping behavior to a greater degree than participants without a serious business problem, b) Participants with a serious business problem will utilize the coping behavior of escape avoidance to a greater degree than those participants without a serious business problem, and c) Participants with a serious business problem will seek social support as a coping behavior to a greater extent than those persons without a serious business problem.

Two-way analysis of variance was initially used to test each sub-theorems. The results were not significant for two of the three sub-theorems, and there was no significant interaction between or within groups. To simplify the analysis, t-test comparisons were done.

Results are shown in Table 15. Although these results were in the predicted direction for the use of self-control and escape avoidance coping behaviors, the differences were not significant. The only area in which there was a significant difference in coping behaviors used by entrepreneurs was in the area of seeking social support. Entrepreneurs who had serious business problems engaged in seeking social support as a coping behavior at significantly higher levels than entrepreneurs without serious business problems. Therefore, there is support for this sub-theorem at the .05 level of significance as well as at the .01 level of significance.

Table 15
Theorem #3

Way of Coping	Less Serious Business Problems	More Serious Business Problems	t-test
Self-Controlling	9.52	10.22	-0.69
Seeking Social Support	7.02	9.87	2.6
Escape Avoidance	4.18	5.40	2.96**

$*p <= .05; **p <= .01$

In addition, three theorems regarding other characteristics of Internal versus External Locus of Control were evaluated, a) Subjects with an Internal Locus of Control will have fewer business problems than subjects with an External Locus of Control.

This theorem was tested by comparison of the two locus of control groups on the number of business problems checked by the subjects. There was no significant difference in the number of business problems experienced by those entrepreneurs with an internal locus of control versus those with an external locus of control. Thus, there is no support for this theorem (see Table 16).

Table 16
Theorem IV

	Internal(n=43) Locus of Control	External(n=41) Locus of Control	t test
# Bus. Problems	6.91	6.61	-0.34

*p <= .05; **p <= .01

Theorem V: Subjects with an Internal Locus of Control will have a higher level of satisfaction with their business than subjects with an External Locus of Control.

In order to evaluate this theorem, the two locus of control groups were compared on each of the three specific satisfaction measures, as well as on overall satisfaction. This analysis is shown in Table 17. As can be seen, the results of these t-tests comparisons were not significant, and Theorem V is not supported.

Table 17
Hypothesis #V

	Internal(n=41) Locus of Control	External(9n=43) Locus of Control	t-test
Fin	.02	.24	0.98
Person	.80	.78	-.08
Feeling	.68	.69	.05
Overall Sat.	1.50	1.71	.48

Theorem VI: Subjects with an Internal Locus of Control will have more positive resolutions of business problems than subjects with an External Locus of Control.

Cross tabulation tables were used to assess differences between groups in terms of the outcome of business problems (i.e. effects on the business and level of satisfaction of the entrepreneur). The results were compared using two different sets of 2 x 3 chi-square cross-tabs. As shown in Tables 18 and 19, the results were not significant either for the level of satisfaction of the participants or the effects on the businesses. In both instances the results were in the opposite direction than expected, with the entrepreneurs who had an external locus of control having a slightly higher number of satisfactory outcomes. There is no support for this theorem.

Table 18
Hypothesis VI

Effect of Outcome on Business	Internal Locus of (n=35) Control	External Locus of Control (n=35)
Improved	23 (65.7%)	27 (77.1%)
No Change	10 (28.6%)	7 (20.0%)
Worse	2 (5.7%)	1 (2.9%)

2 X, 2 d.f. = 1.183, ns

Table 19
Theorem VIII

Feelings About Outcome of Problem	Internal Locus of Control	External Locus of Control
Satisfactory	22 (56.4%)	25 (68.4%)
Unsatisfactory	1 (2.6%)	3 (7.9%)
Unresolved	16 (41.0%)	9 (23.7%)

SUPPLEMENTARY ANALYSIS

Correlations between severity and number of business problems with coping behaviors showed several significant relationships. Subjects were found to use the coping behaviors of confrontive coping and accepting responsibility when faced with severe business problems. They also tended to use self controlling and accepting responsibility when handling a number of different business problems. These ways of coping are quite different from the behaviors of other populations. This result provides additional support for the need for further research on black women, in order to understand how they cope and how they differ from other persons in our society. The results of their coping behaviors are shown below in Table 20.

Table 20
Correlations of Business Problems With Ways of Coping

Coping Style	Severity of Problems	Number of Business Problems
Confrontive	.38**	.20
Distancing	.21	.01
Self-Controlling	.20	.24*
Seeking Social Support	.37**	.21
Accepting Responsibility	.29**	.37**
Escape Avoidance	.20	.13
Planful Problem Solving	-.01	-.10
Positive Reappraisal	.14	.09

CHAPTER SUMMARY

The purpose of this study was to explore the relationship between control beliefs and coping behaviors in a sample of black women entrepreneurs. A mailed questionnaire was used to collect the data. Locus of control beliefs were measured with Levenson's Multi-dimensional Locus of Control Scale and coping behaviors were measured with the Folkman and Lazarus Ways of Coping Scale.

Subjects in this study were found to have more externally oriented locus of control beliefs than reported in previous studies.

The mean for the internal sub-scale was 13.71 with a standard deviation of 5.43. The mean for the powerful others sub-scale was 31.04 with standard deviation of 7.55 and for the chance sub-scale of 33.03 with a standard deviation of 7.02. These results show that these businesswomen are quite externally oriented. While not significant, the results suggest that subjects with an external locus of control tended to cope more effectively, to have larger enterprises, and to derive more satisfaction from owning their own business.

Results did not support the theorem that control beliefs can explain the variance in coping behaviors. A significant correlation was found between seeking social support and the severity of business problems. Overall, results indicate that both control beliefs and coping behaviors of the black women in this study differ from the participants in other studies.

VI

Discussion and Implications

While previous studies have found that variations in locus of control beliefs significantly influence coping behavior, there were no studies in the literature addressing this issue among samples of black women entrepreneurs. This project was developed to address this gap in the literature by assessing the effects of variation in locus of control on the coping behaviors of black women entrepreneurs.

DISCUSSION OF FINDINGS

Participants in this study were all previously employed individuals who had started their own businesses. They apparently had enough confidence in themselves to leave secure jobs and invest their personal assets to start new enterprises which might or might not succeed. Previous studies have found that such persons score high on internal locus of control measures and low on control by luck or powerful others (Rotter, 1966, 1971; Levenson, 1973, 1974). However, the findings did not support the results of previous studies, with the subjects of this study being largely externally oriented. Explanation of this unexpected result must begin with careful re-examination of study variables, analysis of the populations in previous studies, and peculiar characteristics of the subjects in this study.

Many researchers have found that external control is multi-dimensional (Abramowitz, 1973; Levenson, 1973, 1974, 1975; Mirels, 1970). More recently, the dimensionality of internal control has also been questioned (Irion & Blanchard Fields, 1987). Such challenges are important in that they not only lead to further refinement and improved accuracy of instruments, but also force researchers to remain cognizant of the complexity of the theoretical construct.

81

Varying results, using different sample populations, underscore the necessity of determining norms, reliability, and validity on commonly used psychological measurements for specific populations. In-depth analysis of such standard measures of intelligence and psychopathology as the Stanford Binet and the MMPI have found that these measures are influenced by the differences in environmental factors for black persons (Gynthen & Lachar, 1978; Gurin, Gurin, Lao, & Beattre, 1972; Jenkins, 1982).

In addition, data gathered and analyzed in this study goes beyond that which has previously been available, and provides a resource for use in hypothesis development and testing of larger randomized samples. The methodology in a randomized sample produces results that could be generalized to a wider population of black women entrepreneurs, thus improving the quality and breadth of our theoretical and clinical knowledge.

Empirical researchers have generally assumed that individuals can be categorized as either externally or internally oriented (Folkman & Lazarus, 1984; Rotter, 1966; Levenson, 1973a, 1973b). However, measurements of individual control beliefs in natural settings may not be straightforward. Just as a number of researchers began to question the multi-dimensionality of the external component of the Rotter E-I Scale, more recently, some researcher have begun to consider that the internal scale may also have more than one dimension. For example, Irion and Blanchard-Fields (1987) found that individuals tended to become more externally oriented as they grew older, while still retaining much of the internality found in younger persons.

Another explanation for the unexpected results is that there are age differences between the subjects in this study and many of the samples on which norms for the various locus of control instruments were established. Most studies on locus of control have utilized undergraduate students who are both young and inexperienced with the external realities of being completely economically independent (Abramonwitz, 1973; Mirels, 1970; Levenson, 1973). They occupy a relatively favorable position in the social structure, have experienced few hardships, and their basic needs are routinely met. In addition, many subjects in other locus of control studies have been white males and females (Baumgardner, Heppner, & Arkin, 1986; Cooper, 1982;

Kobasa, Maddi, & Courington, 1981; Parkes, 1984). The instruments which were developed to measure control beliefs have been found to be valid and reliable for those populations (Rotter, 1966; Levenson, 1974, 1975).

Studies by Blanchard-Fields and Robinson (1987) and Irion and Blanchard-Fields (1987) found that adolescents and young adults scored much higher on internal measures of locus of control than middle-aged and older subjects. Older subjects also were more external while maintaining many aspects of internal control orientations. Their findings, results of this study, and other researchers suggest that locus of control beliefs are dynamic and adaptive rather than static. The subjects of this study, who have been found to have a mixture of internal and external beliefs, may be quite similar to other adults who are grappling with the problems of the real world. Their scores on the locus of control measure may reflect the complex ever changing quality of many adaptive coping mechanisms. These findings suggest different approaches to studying locus of control beliefs be explored, including longitudinal studies on the same subjects from different ethnic groups.

The conceptual framework of the current study may have failed to adequately account for the interaction of experiences and beliefs with locus of control during the appraisal process. As discussed in Chapter 2, there is solid evidence that there has been a pervasive pattern of discrimination against both blacks and women, and the subjects of this study may have been subjected to both racial and sexual disadvantages which influenced their locus of control beliefs. Their experiences may have made it necessary for them to be more attentive to environmental factors for effective functioning.

More than 80 percent of the subjects reported substantial use of prayer as a coping behavior. Folkman and Lazarus (1980, 1984, 1986) reported that the majority of their subjects used both emotion focused and problem-focused coping, which suggests that the use of prayer does not necessarily indicate a passivity or the absence of active coping behaviors. It does, however, support the literature which portrays black women's coping abilities as being enhanced by the presence of strong religious faith. The influence of black cultural values has led many black women to develop a deep and abiding religious faith which assumes that the "Will of God" is operative in most situations. This view may lead to a acceptance of unfavorable outcome with less distress for black women entrepreneurs in a similar manner as explained by Barbarin (1983) and Neff (1985) in their studies on coping by black persons without diminishing other coping efforts.

One of the psychological defenses that black persons have employed in order to continue striving in a negative environment is to use different explanations for their successes and failures (Neff, 1985; Myers, 1980). Statements such as "I have often found that what is going to happen will happen" may serve as a protection from worry by black persons operating in a racist society. Black persons have been able to attribute differences in their personal circumstances to inequities in the social system (Neff, 1985). Subjects who score high on the C scale may function effectively because they are not afraid of personal failure and are more concerned about the lack of personal effort. The only way to know what is being measured by the statements in the Levenson scales would be to follow up with personal interviews, which are outside of the scope of this study.

There are a number of reasons for different results in this study than previous studies. The norms for these black women entrepreneurs are not necessarily the same as for subjects of other empirical studies which were done largely on young subjects of the majority population (Gurin, Gurin, Lao, & Beattrem 1972). The participants in this study are older and are struggling to deal with the realities of the business world. For them, being successful or reaching their desired goals depended as much on their ability to comprehend the functioning of other individuals and the institutions in the majority society as having ability and intelligence themselves (Gurin, Gurin, Lao, & Beattree, 1972). As black women growing up in the United States, they encountered significant degrees of discrimination and prejudice, creating an overall environment which could be characterized as ranging from unresponsive to negative (Ladner, 1971; Lewis, 1977; Lykes, 1983). In short, the experiences and environments of study participants were significantly different from those of the normed group, and it is quite reasonable to expect that they would develop different beliefs about how to interact effectively in the society.

The selection of specific coping behaviors by the participants in this study was unrelated to their locus of control scores, which is consistent with other studies (Irion & Blanchard-Fields, 1987; Lazarus and Folkman, 1984; McCrae, 1984; Parkes, 1984). Control beliefs are only one element shaping the appraisals made by individual, and may be more helpful in determining general tendencies rather in predicting specific efforts.

With regard to the seriousness of business problems, findings were consistent with previous studies. When subjects made an appraisal that stakes were high (i.e. that the business itself was at risk), a large proportion utilized the coping behavior of seeking social support. Even under these circumstances, however, the research hypothesis was only partially supported. Instead of engaging in escape-avoidance and self-control behaviors, subjects utilized confrontive and accepting responsibility coping behaviors. This difference in coping behaviors may be attributed to the large number of financial transactions inherent in business operations. Folkman and colleagues (1986) found that more confrontive coping was utilized in situations involving financial resources.

Most subjects (67%) reported that the business problem was resolved with a satisfactory outcome. The high number of successful outcomes may be due in part to secondary efforts to handle the problem. It would appear that their coping methods were effective, even though the particular coping behaviors may have differed from those found to be effective in other coping studies.

Discussion of the Sample

The participants ranged in age from 27 years to 70 years. Most had grown up in the Southern states during the period when blacks were legally segregated in schools, jobs, public accommodations, and many other areas of their daily lives. Despite this background, the majority went to college and half earned graduate degrees. A large majority of the subjects had been employed before starting their businesses, with only eight subjects having been housewives or unemployed. Previous jobs were largely middle level clerical and administrative position, often in public school systems.

The study sample consisted primarily of highly educated and assertive women living in California. These black women, largely educated as school teachers and clerical workers, chose to seek greater financial rewards and personal freedom in part due to favorable environmental factors supportive of business ownership by minorities and women. The financial rewards derived from their businesses were also strongly influenced by environmental factors, as reflected in the fact that type of business was more predictive of gross receipts than either length of time in business or educational level.

Characteristics of the customer base of the entrepreneurs' businesses demonstrates the effect of societal changes on business viability. The majority of the entrepreneurs reported that their customers came from the general public rather than from the black community. The black women whose businesses catered primarily to the black community mentioned a lack of patronage, as well as a perceived inability or unwillingness by black customers to pay for the products or services. The subjects with the most financially successful businesses were those who competed for their share of the general market, and whose businesses were representative of the range and scope of enterprises found in their area.

Profile of Typical Subject

The typical black woman entrepreneur was born in the South, but her parents came to California when she was just a toddler. She is the oldest of four children and has been encouraged by her parents to get a "good education as a requirement for getting a good job." She continued to work after she was married and had her child. Things did not change very much for her after she got her divorce. Her family had always assisted with the care of her son and provided more help for her than her husband. She had been reared to have a deep faith in God, to believe that she could do anything that she really wanted to do, to provide for her family, and to meet her responsibilities. She believes that whatever ever was going to happen, was going to happen, and what was for you, you would get. She prays often for God to give her strength and patience to do what she has to do. She scored high on the external measures of locus of control and she believes that she must know a lot about how the world, institutions, and society works if she expects to be successful. Yet, she believes that what happens in her life depends on her efforts and continued hard work.

The typical subject is a divorced woman in her late thirties or early forties. She has one adult child. She is a sole proprietor and she operates a professional or personal service business. She started the business with her own savings. One or two family members work in the business with her and are strong sources of social support as well as material help.

Our typical entrepreneur has a graduate degree. She was employed as a middle manager before opening her own business. She became frustrated at her lack of advancement into the higher ranks and the subtle undermining of her authority by higher level administrators or the prejudiced behavior of sub-ordinates.

She is very satisfied with her business. She started the business with encouragement from her family and friends. However, she knew very little about financial business practices or how to find new customers, after the first group of old customers and friends were not enough to make the business a financial success. She also under-estimated the amount of work and time involved in owning your own business. Her income is greater than when she was working for someone else, but she lacks the business skills to expand her enterprise beyond it's present capacity. She is experiencing her biggest problems with irregular cash flow, canceled orders, and failure of some customers to pay for services. She is in need of specialized training, a formal and informal business contacts, and additional financial resources.

Influence of the Family

Not surprisingly, the immediate family has an impact on the entrepreneur's ability to cope with the multiple roles of family life and business ownership. Married subjects generally had spouses who were extremely supportive. In addition to representing sources of social support, many subjects had family members as partners, investors and employees.

Findings of the study also demonstrate the importance of the family of origin. The importance of having a parent who was self-employed, which has been found in studies of majority entrepreneurs, was confirmed. Results showed that 44.3 percent of fathers and 24.6 percent of mothers had owned and operated their own businesses. The relatively high educational level of the subjects can probably be attributed to family values of achievement and support for their efforts. Many of the subjects also had parents who were professionals or college educated, thus providing daily role models and "know-how" for successfully interacting with the environment. Although the majority of the subjects were born in the South, most now live and operate their businesses in the West, which is indicative of their desire for a better economic life and of their ability to cope with and overcome societal factors to achieve a better economic life.

The systematic use of the locus of control construct and the various instruments which measure control beliefs will continue to be important. Developing an understanding of psychological factors and the ability to predict behavior is of paramount interest to social scientists, and theory development and testing are the primary methods through which such knowledge is gained and made available for clinical use.

It is important that additional studies of black women entrepreneurs be done. Each additional study can be used to refine hypotheses as black women entrepreneurs interact with various situations in their business and personal environment. There is no basis for the assumptions that norms developed for the majority population are applicable to this population, and continued studies are needed to establish a base of knowledge specific to black women entrepreneurs.

Successful operation of a business requires many entrepreneurial qualities, one of the most important being self-knowledge by the entrepreneur regarding what her role should be during every phase of business (i.e. start-up, survival, and growth). The use of locus of control concepts is a major tool for helping professions when assessing the potential of black women for self direction and in evaluating their use of adequate coping strategies. Knowledge of how other successful black women entrepreneurs have scored on various measures of locus of control would be valuable to potential, new, or troubled black women entrepreneurs.

Results of this study suggest a pressing need to examine the effects of environment on locus of control beliefs. The subjects in this study (in contrast to most previous studies with non-minority samples) grew up in and live in a racist and sexist environment that is unresponsive to individual needs. This alone may be an important factor in explaining the fact that these women did not conform to the hypothesized image derived from previous research.

Directions for Future Research

This study shared the weakness of many studies on black women in that it did not address the problems which result from discrimination against ethnic groups and females. No data were collected on subjects' experiences with discrimination and sexism in starting or operating their businesses. Future studies should include data on both the types of discrimination problems encountered and the coping behaviors utilized. For example, subjects could complete the Ways of Coping instrument for problems which they appraised as deriving from racism or sexism or racism and sexism, and then again for more general business problems.

One possible problem with this study was the non-random nature of the sample and the possibility that a response bias existed. These black women were highly motivated and successful in their own businesses, as well as assertive and self-confident. Ninety percent of the subjects were from California, and three-fourths held college degrees. Most of them held administrative jobs prior to going into business, and most reported a strong network of family and social support. These characteristics suggest that the study sample was probably not representative of the larger population of black women who have started their own businesses across the United States. Generalizations from the results of this study may not be applicable to black women entrepreneurs with different background characteristics.

This study was limited by the absence of a personal interview with the participants. At least one personal interview would have enabled the researcher to develop a better understanding of the appraisal process. The study would have been greatly enhanced by in-depth interviews regarding the commitments, values and views of black businesswomen. The section on business problems could have yielded stronger results if participants had been asked to describe and rank the serious business problems which they had encountered since starting their business.

The findings of this study make clear the need for further research on the locus of control psychological construct in black populations. One problem with such research is that available methodologies have been developed and validated utilizing samples of white men and women, and may or may not be appropriate for studying minority samples. Since the construct is influenced by environmental and cultural factors, it is important that present day acceptance of the construct as relating only to personality characteristics be challenged by the existence of empirically obtained data. The objective of such research would be to explore and confirm if and how locus of control beliefs differs among various populations, including blacks and whites. It is only by additional studies that either new norms will be established for black persons and other minorities or the measures of locus control will be modified to included supplementary factors which will make the measurement of the construct more accurate and useful.

The research conducted for this study demonstrated the complexities of utilizing literature from diverse social science disciplines. The literature from such diverse fields as business, sociology, psychology, social work, and women's and black studies is diverse, and does not utilize the same vocabulary or techniques. Each discipline has its own concepts, language, and ways of formulating and testing theories.

Utilizing literature from such diverse fields also creates the problem of analyzing the multiple levels of theories and concepts. Some of the commonly encountered differences were the contrasts between writings at the macro systems level as compared to the micro level. Various theories and approaches address the individual, formal and informal groups, various segments of the society, or the entire society. Even when issues addressed were at the individual level, some focused on psychological, while others looked at social or physical problems. The state of knowledge in the social sciences makes resolution of these problems impossible at this time.

This study also demonstrated the problems inherent in conducting empirical research on highly theoretical concepts. The concepts of locus of control, stress and coping are elaborately formulated, but not completely understood by previous theorists and empirical researchers in their respective fields (Folkman, 1980). These theories are under continual development and refinement, and the instruments used to measure the concepts are crude in contrast to the complexity of human nature (Parkes, 1984). When concepts are operationalized as variables, the concepts may be inadequately captured and may or may not measure the aspects that the researchers intended. Even when instruments work well in one study or with some populations, they may not be reliable in predicting specific behaviors. Also, the instrument used to measure ways of coping has been found to be more satisfactory when tied more closely to the stressful event and when repeated measurements are done.

This study demonstrates that black women have considerable variety in their control beliefs, with those who are more external or who have better understanding of society seeming to function better. These women have developed many coping behaviors that serve them well, and which are similar to those used by other black women (i.e. social support and religious faith). Their family ties are strong, with many family members involved in their business. Some of the entrepreneurs experienced problems of negative social support from the black community, friends, and some family members. A certain number of these entrepreneurs were without any sources of support and would almost certainly be helped by informal business networks and formal mentors.

The primary implication of this study of black women may be that it illustrates that there are many paths to adequate functioning. The levels of tasks or stressors do not indicate the level of stress experienced or the level of coping behaviors required of an individual. Similarly, the volume of coping activities does not necessarily determine satisfactory or unsatisfactory outcomes. Situational factors are central in any coping episode and can only be understood by the meaning that the entrepreneur attaches to it. Comments made by some of the entrepreneurs indicated that they had not resolved the place of the business in their lives, especially relative to other important roles. While much was learned, this study generated as many questions as were answered. The study clearly demonstrates that we remain at the very beginning level of inquiry in our knowledge of black women entrepreneurs.

Implications of the Study

The results of this study strongly suggest that greater attention needs to be paid to the role played by personal values and religion in the appraisals of black women. Black women seem to be able to combine commitment with traditional family roles, while still maintaining strong involvement in business and career. The function of religious convictions may be to provide black women with the confidence to persevere in stressful situations. With regard to specific coping behaviors, it is quite important to examine situational variables. Data obtained in this study show clearly that the participants are coping with many roles and situations simultaneously.

There is an extensive body of literature supporting the proposition that an internal locus of control has positive effects for the individual (Rotter, 1966, 1971; Kobasa, Maddi & Courington, 1981; Kobasa, Maddi & Zola 1983; Mirels, 1970; Levenson, 1973, 1974, 1975; Abramovitz, 1973; Parkes, 1984). Among the factors identified are an increased ability to cope with stressful life events with fewer mood disturbances, to maintain better mental and physical health, and to maintain firm commitments to stated goals. However, the failure of the empirical researchers to included a substantial numbers of persons from various ethnic minorities, age groups, and classes has led to some misleading results.

The norms established on various locus of control measures are based primarily on young white subjects. The findings in those studies that persons, who scored higher on the internal measures of control were also more capable, competent, and effective has led to the generalization that to have an internal locus of control is preferable to having an external locus of control. This preference for "internals", when automatically applied to individuals from groups who have not been included in those studies and for whom norms have not been established, amounts to a prejudiced and biased use of the findings, if minority or other persons do not score similarly to the groups on which the norm was established.

Few studies refer to the use of specific coping efforts or outcomes, and the studies that have attempted to link control beliefs to specific coping behaviors have not found a significant correlation (Irion & Blanchard-Fields, 1987; McCrae 1984; Parkes, 1984). The link between specific behaviors, successful or satisfactory outcomes, and locus of control scores has not been established, as many professionals assume. Further empirical studies of specific behaviors and locus of control measures will have to be done in order for an accurate determination of the relationship between the variables to be made. Many of the existing studies serve to misguide professionals who think that they can make meaningful selections of individuals to recommend for vocational programs based on locus of control scores, when in fact most of the locus of control instruments do not correlate highly with specific behaviors or predict successful resolutions (Lazarus & Folkman, 1984). Psychological theorists and empirical researchers have an obligation to proceed cautiously when applying the results of their studies to the general population. Such automatic assumptions that persons who score differently from whites are not as able or capable of being successful have the dangers, although on a much smaller scale, of repeating the earlier "scientific" mistakes of the superiority of the Aryan races (Gould, 1981).

Implications for Social Workers

In working with black female clients, social workers should be aware that their behavior may not be predicted by commonly used psychological tests. Norms which have been developed for most published instruments were established using quite different populations, and the validity of the even the best-known instruments for this specific population should not be assumed. When using the locus of control scores of black women, in counselling regarding future career goals, the measures should be used primarily as a starting place to discuss the clients views of the world, society, and how various formal systems and institutions work. Used in this manner social workers will be able to discern if the clients are knowledgeable, astute, or simplistic and naive. Social workers can find out if clients are able and willing to work hard to achieve stated goals or if their beliefs about what happens to a person is such that very little effort or creativity is likely to come forth. Also, such discussions can aid social workers in learning whether the black woman has been frustrated by the obstacles in the labor market, although she possesses the education, skills and ambitions to succeed on her own.

It is more important for social workers to constantly gather information regarding the values, experiences, and beliefs of clients than it is to automatically administer a battery of tests which have questionable practical value. Agencies' utilization of locus of control measurement instruments to aid staff in the selection of candidates for programs must be done cautiously and only in conjunction with other psychological measurements, assessment tools, interviews, and background information. The most important assessment and selection tool for social workers, in making an important decision on the future life and career of clients of different ethnic groups is knowledge the culture, values, views, and experiences of those clients. This knowledge, coupled with good judgement and the ability to weigh all the pertinent factors as they relate to specific clients, will lead to good selections of entrepreneurial candidates in the majority of the cases.

Recommended Action Agencies working with black women considering life changes, career, or educational programs should incorporate self-assessment techniques for their clients. This would involve assessment of (a) life and career goals, (b) experiences and reaction to discrimination, sexism, and bias, and (c) evaluation of available resources.

Implications for Social Work Education

Social work students should develop an awareness of the risks inherent in applying theories of what is "normal" in the general population to subgroups with much different backgrounds. This is certainly the case with black women, both in terms of academic analysis and practical social work. Graduate programs should place greater emphasis on the need to take the client's point of view, and to make objective assessments without imposing inappropriate assumptions or models. Students need to develop the ability to assess the client's coping resources and abilities if they hope to be of real help to them.

Social work students who will be working with black families need to understand the cultural and social context, and especially the nature of the economic situation faced by black women. The standard remedies which have been proposed for helping black women include such things as education and training in fields already dominated by females, and which are both overcrowded and low paying (e.g. clerical work). These fields hold little promise for a fulfilling career, and often consist of little more than boring, dead end jobs. Social work students need to gain at least a working knowledge of alternative jobs and career paths which are expanding and have the potential for a meaningful and rewarding career. Entrepreneurship, of course, represents an important option which is all too often ignored or even discouraged by naive social workers who fail to realize how appropriate such an option can be for black women.

Recommended Action Universities should establish an academic requirement which necessitates that every master level social work student take a minimum of one course of business, vocational, or career counseling. Alternatively, the schools of social work should develop and incorporate in its curriculum the aforementioned requirement.

Implications for Industrial Social Work

Students entering the field of industrial social work, which has enjoyed a resurgence in recent years, should definitely be made aware of these issues. Courses in Industrial Social Work programs should provide information and perspective on settings beyond that of industry or corporate settings. Students should develop a base of knowledge about the various entrepreneurial programs, services of economic development agencies, and Small Business Administration resources. Many black women become frustrated with their careers in the corporate setting, and develop a desire for independence and control over their own careers. Referrals to these agencies for evaluation and assistance may open up many options and alternatives which simply did not exist in years past.

Recommended Action Establish regular seminars and open forums in which professionals from the community come in to share their experiences. Representatives from various professions could discuss training, obstacles, credentials, salaries, and so forth. Additionally, an internship program should be established in which industrial social work students spend one semester or quarter working and learning in scientific, technical, or industrial firms.

Implications for Child Welfare and School Social Work

Students in these specialties will probably work with black women from a disadvantaged socio-economic background. Many such clients have little or no education or work history, and the social worker is constantly challenged to find ways to intervene in such a way as to break the vicious circle of poverty. These students can be taught to make contacts with local business and professional associations, sororities and community groups which can be utilized to identify successful black females who can serve as valuable role models. There are also a number of associations of black entrepreneurs that could be encouraged to make volunteer or part-time positions available for black female adolescents. This would serve the dual purposes of providing poor black females with positive role models and helping them develop a sense of competence and self-esteem.

Recommended Action Faculty members of the various schools of social work should be appointed to work with black women's business and professional organizations to establish work site tours, career days, and sponsorship linkages for disadvantaged black female adolescents, which could include not only mentor type relationships but also part-time and summer jobs.

Implications for Black Families

Ideally, black families should provide a warm and supportive environment for their female children; optimal development requires a sense of freedom, individuality, and imagination from the earliest age. Parents should continue to teach their female children to be self-reliant, encourage them to complete their education, and to pursue their own careers. However, it is also important that business ownership be seen as a desirable and viable option in contrast to the present emphasis on getting a "good job" working from someone else. Parents should make an effort to expose their children to black female role models working in a wide range of careers, with emphasis on the non-traditional careers. The rationale behind such a step is to provide greater perspective on the full range of career options available to black women versus continuing to focus exclusively on the traditional paths to economic success. Parents should also strive to present a balanced picture of the relationship between each individual and his or her environment. Children should be taught that what happens to individuals and families depends to a large degree on how they treat themselves and one another. The pervasive negative atmosphere of powerlessness and despair characteristic of many urban areas can be replaced by an awareness that each of us has important choices to make, and that those choices play a significant role in determining what happens to us in life.

Recommended Action In addition to parents pointing to the successes of media celebrities and professional athletes, they also need to advise their children of the limited number of such positions available even for the most skilled and talented person. Parents should educate themselves and their children on the occupational fields that are growing and expanding, which will provide opportunities for economic self sufficiency and career advancement in the future. They should seek out black women who have succeeded in business ownership as well as scientific and non-traditional careers as role models for their daughters.

Implications for the Black Community

Informal networks in the black community play an important role as a social support for both black female entrepreneurs and for black women seeking to start their own businesses. In addition to good will, formal networks can provide information and business expertise through social, community, and religious organizations. Many of the women who start businesses are poorly equipped to meet the many problems they inevitably face. Professional groups can establish connections with local minority business development departments to get information. Organizations can also sponsor workshops, business fairs, and economic development forums to assist entrepreneurs in their struggle to become less isolated and more knowledgeable.

Recommended Action Sororities, business, professional, and social organizations should co-sponsor seminars and workshops for ministers and church organizations to help them understand the relationship of anti-business attitudes to the problems encountered by local black-owned businesses. These workshops should stress the importance of cooperative economic ventures and financial investment in black enterprises. Churches should be encouraged to establish income-generating ventures which could provide learning and employment opportunities for black adolescents.

Implications for the Broader Community

Formal organizations, ranging from school systems to Chambers of Commerce, should also provide services to black female entrepreneurs. Of course, black women must also take the initiative by becoming involved in community activities. These linkages are crucial if the organizations are to become aware of their responsibilities and the black women to become aware of the resources that are available.

Recommended Action Each of the forums mentioned above should be open to members of the broader community, including chambers of commerce, community colleges, and public agencies.

Implications for Vocational Schools and Colleges

There is an urgent need for vocational schools and colleges to address the problems faced by black women. The subjects in the current study were for the most part trained as teachers and school administrators, which reflects the sex role stereotyping which permeates our educational system. Better counseling and guidance beginning in high school could have prevented these women, and many others like them, from spending years in preparation for a career that was not really suited to their personalities.

Recommended Action   Each vocational school and college should require their black women clients to attend business expositions, job fairs, and conferences. They should also attend job recruitment weekends sponsored by large corporations, computer and technical firms, and universities.

Implications for Governmental Agencies

Public sector agencies at all levels need to become more involved in addressing the problems faced by black female entrepreneurs. Federal agencies, and in particular the Small Business Administration, offer many valuable programs for small business operators; however, due to the lack of systematic outreach, many black females remain unaware that such programs even exist. Media advertising could be utilized to advise small business owners of the availability of informational workshops, technical assistance, financing, and consultation.

Recommended Action   Policies should be modified to encourage black women to seek employment in non-traditional fields, including self-employment. Services should be advertised on daytime television programs and radio stations which target the black community.

CONCLUSION

The position of black women entrepreneurs can perhaps best be expressed in broad, systems level terms. The comprehensive social environment has a series of formal and informal organizations and groups, which represent both resources for coping and obstacles to be overcome. The individual is affected by all of the various systems at one level or another. The interaction of the women in this study with the broader environment at all levels had an impact in shaping and modifying their beliefs about control in their lives. Their control beliefs differed from what one might expect based on textbooks or conventional knowledge. Although the sample in this study was relatively small and not necessarily representative of the broader population of black women entrepreneurs, the subjects were clearly women with tremendous drive and highly developed coping abilities. They showed an ability to adapt to the requirements of the dominant culture, and utilized effective coping strategies to deal with the many stressors in their environment. To achieve this, they relied on coping resources such as their knowledge of the environment, intelligence, past occupational experience, and social support networks. That they have "made it" as independent business owners provides evidence that it is indeed possible for segments of our diverse population to attain success on their own terms. Nevertheless, the success of black women entrepreneurs has been gained only after surmounting tremendous obstacles, and as yet remain grossly under represented among the total population of entrepreneurs.

APPENDIX A
QUESTIONNAIRE

Sch# _____

Personal Data

---

1. Sex
    ___ male   ___ *female*
2. Age_____
3. Marital Status: (check one)
    ___ *single*   ___ *married*
    ___ *divorced/separated*   ___ *widow/widower*
4. Number of your own children _____   Age Range _____
Number living at home _____
5. Education: (check highest)
    ___ *less than 9 years*   ___ *9-11 years*
    ___ *high school graduate*   ___ *some college*
    ___ *college degree*   ___ graduate or professional
    ___ *technical or specialized training*
6. Your occupation prior to starting business _____

Family Background

---

1. Birth Place
                            State/Country _____
2. No. of sisters __
3. You were child number ___ in your family
4. Father's occupation _____
    a. *owned business or self employed yes __ or no __*
    b. *education level* _____
5. Mother's occupation _____
    a. *owned business or self employed yes __ or no __*
    b. *education level* _____

Sch# _____

Personal Beliefs

Directions: Read each statement below. Think about the statement and decide if you STRONGLY AGREE WITH, AGREE WITH IT, DISAGREE WITH IT, or STRONGLY DISAGREE WITH IT. Then circle the words on the right that best describes how you feel.

1. Whether or not I get to be a leader depends mostly on my ability.   STRONGLY AGREE   AGREE   DISAGREE   STRONGLY DISAGREE

2. To a great extent my life is controlled by accidental happenings.   STRONGLY AGREE   AGREE   DISAGREE   STRONGLY DISAGREE

3. I feel like what happens in my life is mostly determined by powerful people.   STRONGLY AGREE   AGREE   DISAGREE   STRONGLY DISAGREE

4. Whether on not I get into a car accident depends mostly on how good a driver I am.   STRONGLY AGREE   AGREE   DISAGREE   STRONGLY DISAGREE

5. When I make plans, I am almost certain to make them work.   STRONGLY AGREE   AGREE   DISAGREE   STRONGLY DISAGREE

Sch# _____

6. Often there   STRONGLY   AGREE   DISAGREE   STRONGLY
is no chance of AGREE   DISAGREE
protecting my
personal interest
from bad luck
happenings.

7. When I get   STRONGLY   AGREE   DISAGREE   STRONGLY
what I want, it's AGREE   DISAGREE
usually because
I'm lucky.

8. Although I   STRONGLY   AGREE   DISAGREE   STRONGLY
might have good AGREE   DISAGREE
ability, I will not
be given
leadership
responsibility
without
appealing to
those in
positions of
power.

9. How many   STRONGLY   AGREE   DISAGREE   STRONGLY
friends I have   AGREE   DISAGREE
depends on how
nice a person I
am.

10. I have often STRONGLY   AGREE   DISAGREE   STRONGLY
found that what AGREE   DISAGREE
is going to
happen will
happen.

11. My life is   STRONGLY   AGREE   DISAGREE   STRONGLY
chiefly   AGREE   DISAGREE
controlled by
powerful others.

12. Whether or   STRONGLY   AGREE   DISAGREE   STRONGLY
not I get into a AGREE   DISAGREE
car accident is
mostly a matter
of luck.

Sch# _____

13. People like STRONGLY   AGREE   DISAGREE   STRONGLY
myself have very AGREE   DISAGREE
little chance of
protecting our
personal
interests when
they conflict
with those of
strong pressure
groups.

14. It's not   STRONGLY   AGREE   DISAGREE   STRONGLY
always wise for AGREE   DISAGREE
me to plan too
far ahead
because many
things turn out
to be a matter
of good or bad
fortune.

15. Getting   STRONGLY   AGREE   DISAGREE   STRONGLY
what I want   AGREE   DISAGREE
requires
pleasing those
people above
me.

16. Whether or STRONGLY   AGREE   DISAGREE   STRONGLY
not I get to be a AGREE   DISAGREE
leader depends
on whether I'm
lucky enough to
be in the right
place at the
right time.

17. If important STRONGLY AGREE   DISAGREE   STRONGLY
people were to   AGREE   DISAGREE
decide they
didn't like me. I
probably
wouldn't make
many friends.

18. I can pretty much determine what will happen in my life. **STRONGLY AGREE**   **AGREE**   **DISAGREE**   **STRONGLY DISAGREE**

Sch# _____

19. I am usually able to protect my personal interests. **STRONGLY AGREE**   **AGREE**   **DISAGREE**   **STRONGLY DISAGREE**

20. Whether or not I get into a car accident depends mostly on the other driver. **STRONGLY AGREE**   **AGREE**   **DISAGREE**   **STRONGLY DISAGREE**

21. When I get what I want, it's usually because I worked hard for it. **STRONGLY AGREE**   **AGREE**   **DISAGREE**   **STRONGLY DISAGREE**

22. In order to have my plans work, I make sure that they fit in with the desires of people who have power over me. **STRONGLY AGREE**   **AGREE**   **DISAGREE**   **STRONGLY DISAGREE**

23. My life is determined by my own actions. **STRONGLY AGREE**   **AGREE**   **DISAGREE**   **STRONGLY DISAGREE**

24. It's chiefly a matter of fate whether or not I have a few friends or many friends. **STRONGLY AGREE**   **AGREE**   **DISAGREE**   **STRONGLY DISAGREE**

Sch# _____

Description of Business

The following questions gather information on the description of your business. Please answer the questions regarding the business from which you receive your major income.

1. Year you started the business _____
2. Locations: city _____ and state _____
3. Type of business (check one)
    __ automobile dealership/service station
    __ construction/building trade
    __ food stores
    __ services (__*professional*__*personal*__*technical*)
    __ manufacturing
    __ restaurant/bar
    __ retail
    __ trucking/transportation
    __ wholesale
    __ other _____

4. Business ownership
    __ sole proprietor
    __ limited partnership
    __ general partnership
    __ closed corporation
    __ publicly held corporation
    __ franchise

5. Size of business
    __ number of employees
    __ number of family/relatives employed in the business
    __ number of separate business locations
    gross receipts for last year _____

6. Other business interests
    (a) Was this your first business? yes ___   no ___
    (b) Do you own, operate, or have financial interests in another business? yes ___   no ___

Sch# _____

Customer Profile

The majority of my customers are (check one for each questions):

1. Ethnicity
   ___ Blacks   ___ Blacks and other minorities
   ___ Whites   ___ Equally Black and White
   ___ General Public

2. Service Area
   ___ Local (city wide)   ___ National
   ___ Regional (counties)   ___ International
   ___ Statewide

3. Income
   ___ Below $15,000   ___ $25,000 - $49,999
   ___ $15,000 - $24,999   ___ $50,000 and above

Business Support

Think back to the period before you started your business and answer the following questions:

1. When I told individuals regarding my plan to go into business for myself, they reacted: (please check one)
   favorable/supportive   negative/discouraging
   (a) spouse_____   _____
   (b) parents_____   _____
   (c) siblings_____   _____
   (d) friends_____   _____
2. My biggest moral supporter and booster was _____

3. Sources of finances to begin the business was (check all that apply)
   ___ personal savings and assets
   ___ loans from family members and relatives
   ___ loans from non-related individuals (investors)
   ___ loans from banks and other financial institutions
   ___ other _____

Sch# _____

Business Problems

The next group of questions are regarding business problems you have encountered at any time since being in business. Check all that apply.

1. Money
   ___ unable to get financing/credit to start
   ___ underestimated amount needed to get started
   ___ cashflow problems - sales or income irregular
   ___ business slow to produce income
   ___ not enough capital to expand business to increase production or to obtain larger facilities
   ___ too much money spent in specific areas, such as inventory or space
   ___ trucking/transportation
2. Customers
   ___ little knowledge of how to reach potential new customers
   ___ wrong location and inconvenient for customers
   ___ no marketing or advertising plan
   ___ advertising ineffective
3. Sales
   ___ slow
   ___ high/old accounts receivable
   ___ too many sales
   ___ orders canceled
   ___ bad debt
   ___ unable to deliver on time
4. Equipment/Supplies
   ___ too costly
   ___ wrong kind
   ___ unavailable
   ___ maintenance problems
5. Labor
   ___ skilled labor not available
   ___ labor cost underestimated
   ___ job not clear, responsibility and tasks overlaps and gaps
   ___ personnel policies and practices
   ___ skilled labor too expensive
   ___ staff conflicts
6. Business Organization
   ___ written business plan
   ___ several services/departments competing for resources
   ___ growth or development criteria
   ___ authority structure
   ___ goals of the business

7. Ownership Problems
   __ non-working partners
   __ how to assign equity/salaries
   __ maintaining control of business with investors
   __ disagreements among partners/owners
   __ unable to dissolve partnership
8. Other Problems (please state briefly)_____

Coping

---

1. What staff (persons not directly related to production) have you hired, when? why?

_____

_____

2. The next group of questions we would like for you to answer in relationship to a major specific (one only) business problem which you experienced within the last twelve months.
Please describe the business problem _____

_____

3. Please rank the severity of the above problem to your business, with 1 being very little and 10 being devastating to the business. Please circle your answer.

1 2 3 4 5 6 7 8 9 10

Sch# _____

Please read each item below and indicate, by circling the appropriate category, to what extent you used it in the situation you have just described.

	Not Used	Used some-what	Used quite a bit	Used a great deal
1. Just concentrated on what I had to do next--the next step.	0	1	2	3
2. I tried to analyze the problem in order to understand it better.	0	1	2	3
3. Turned to work or substitute activity to take my mind off things	0	1	2	3
4. I felt that time would make a difference the only thing to do was to wait	0	1	2	3
5. Bargained or compromised to get something positive from the situation.	0	1	2	3
6. I did something which I didn't think would work, but at least I was doing something.	0	1	2	3
7. Tried to get the person responsible to change his or her mind.	0	1	2	3
8. Talked to someone to find out more about the situation.	0	1	2	3
9. Criticized or lectured myself.	0	1	2	3
10. Tried not to burn my bridges, but leave things open somewhat.	0	1	2	3
11. Hoped a miracle would happen.	0	1	2	3
12. Went along with fate; sometimes I just have bad luck.	0	1	2	3

13. Went on as if nothing had happened.	0	1	2	3
14. I tried to keep my feelings to myself.	0	1	2	3
15. Looked for the silver lining, so to speak; tried to look on the bright side of things.	0	1	2	3
16. Slept more than usual.	0	1	2	3
17. I expressed anger to the person(s) who caused the problem.	0	1	2	3
18. Accepted sympathy and understanding from someone.	0	1	2	3
19. I told myself things that helped me to feel better.	0	1	2	3
20. I was inspired to do something creative.	0	1	2	3
21. Tried to forget the whole thing.	0	1	2	3
22. I got professional help.	0	1	2	3
23. Changed or grew as a person in a good way.	0	1	2	3
24. I waited to see what would happen before doing anything.	0	1	2	3
25. I apologized or did something to make up.	0	1	2	3
26. I made a plan of action and followed it.	0	1	2	3
27. I accepted the next best thing to what I wanted.	0	1	2	3
28. I let my feelings out somehow.	0	1	2	3
29. Realized I brought the problem on myself.	0	1	2	3

30. I came out of the experience better than when I went in.	0	1	2	3

30. I came out of the experience better than when I went in.   0   1   2   3

31. Talked to someone who could do something concrete about the problem.   0   1   2   3

32. Got away from it for a while; tried to rest or take a vacation.   0   1   2   3

33. Tried to make myself feel better by eating, drinking, smoking, using drugs or medication, etc.   0   1   2   3

34. Took a big chance or did something very risky.   0   1   2   3

35. I tried not to act too hastily or follow my first hunch.   0   1   2   3

36. Found some new faith.   0   1   2   3

37. Maintained my pride and kept a stiff upper lip.   0   1   2   3

38. Rediscovered what is important in life.   0   1   2   3

39. Changed something so things would turn out all right.   0   1   2   3

40. Avoided being with people in general.   0   1   2   3

41. Didn't let it get to me; refused to think too much about it.   0   1   2   3

42. I asked a relative or friend I respected for advice.   0   1   2   3

43. Dept others from knowing how bad things were.   0   1   2   3

44. Made light of the situation; refused to get too serious about it.   0   1   2   3

	0	1	2	3
45. Talked to someone and fought for what I wanted.	0	1	2	3
46. Stood my ground and fought for what I wanted.	0	1	2	3
47. Took it out on other people.	0	1	2	3
48. Drew on my past experiences; I was in a similar situation before.	0	1	2	3
49. I knew what had to be done, so I doubled my efforts to make things work.	0	1	2	3
50. Refused to believe that it had happened.	0	1	2	3
51. I made a promise to myself that things would be different next time.	0	1	2	3
52. Came up with a couple of different solutions to the problem.	0	1	2	3
53. Accepted it, since nothing could be done.	0	1	2	3
54. I tried to keep my feelings from interfering with other things too much.	0	1	2	3
55. Wished that I could change what had happened or how I felt.	0	1	2	3
56. I changed something about myself.	0	1	2	3
57. I daydreamed or imagined a better time or place than the one I was in.	0	1	2	3
58. Wished that the situation would go away or somehow be over with.	0	1	2	3

59. Had fantasies or wishes about how things might turn out.	0	1	2	3
60. I prayed.	0	1	2	3
61. I prepared myself for the worst.	0	1	2	3
62. I went over in my mind what I would say or do.	0	1	2	3
63. I thought about how a person I admire would handle this situation and used that as a model.	0	1	2	3
64. I tried to see things from the other person's point of view.	0	1	2	3
65. I reminded myself how much worse things could be.	0	1	2	3
66. I jogged or exercised.	0	1	2	3

Resolutions and Feelings

1. Outcome of Problem
   __ satisfactory
   __ unsatisfactory
   __ not resolved

2. Effect of Outcome on Business?
   __ improved
   __ no change
   __ worse

3. Please complete either section A and B regarding the rewards or lack of them in your business. *Please check one in each section.*

   A. Financial Rewards
   __ very profitable
   __ provides a living
   __ constant struggle to pay expenses
   __ have to work another job to supplement business income
   __ thought about quitting business

B. Personal Rewards
__ control over my life and destiny
__ flexible hours
__ business interferes with personal life and relationships
__ business seems to control me instead of me controlling it
__ business has negative on my physical or emotional health

4. Please answer the following questions about your feelings of owning your own business. *Please check one.*

__ I would go into business sooner
__ I would do exactly the same thing
__ I would go into a different business
__ I don't know what I would do
__ I would operate the business part-time and remain employed
__ I would not go into business

Thank You!

Thank you for your time and attention in participating in this study. It is only by persons such as you that this project can be completed.

____ Check here if you would like to receive a copy of the results.

APPENDIX B
INFORMED CONSENT FORM

SUBJECT CONSENT FORM

Title of Project: Control Beliefs and Coping Behaviors Among Black Women Entrepreneurs

Project Director: Lois Harry

This is to certify that I _____
_____ hereby agree to participate as a subject in this research under the supervision of Ms. Harry. The overall purpose of this study is to learn more about black women who found and operate their own businesses. This project will gather information on demographics and other characteristics. It seeks to learn what the problems are that black women entrepreneurs encounter and what they do about the situations. The project will explore the control beliefs of the subjects and how these beliefs affect their coping behaviors.

The following special procedures will be involved:

1. Lois Harry, a doctoral candidate at the University of Southern California, will direct this study with the consultation of Dr. W. Finch, Dr. K. Ell, and Dr. J. Davis, faculty members at USC.

2. There will be a mailed which takes about an half hour to complete which includes questions about beliefs, problems, and coping activities of the subjects.

3. I understand that my voluntary participation or refusal to participate will be kept confidential. The information that I give will be kept confidential. The information that I give will be kept confidential and no information will be reported in any way that could be identified with me.

4. Some of the questions asked may be sensitive and I have the right to refuse to answer them if I find them uncomfortable.

The purpose of the study has been explained to me. I understand that if I have further questions that I may write or telephone Ms. Harry. She will gladly answer any questions that I have regarding the questionnaire or the study.

_____   _____Subjects
signature   Date

APPENDIX C
COVER LETTER TO STUDY
PARTICIPANTS

BLACK WOMEN ENTREPRENEURS QUESTIONNAIRE

March 21, 1988

Dear Participants:

The purpose of this questionnaire is to learn more about black women, who have started and operate their own business. To my knowledge my project is the only academic research on the needs and problems of black business women. It is only by learning more about the actual characteristics of this group and the situations they encounter that programs and services can be realistically designed to encourage more black women to go into business. These programs can also assist new business owners to prepare for the tasks and to handle the problems that they will encounter in operating their own enterprises.

Thank you for taking time to participate in this project. It should only require 30 to 40 minutes to complete. Your answer will be kept confidential. No information will given to anyone that could be identifying as coming from you.

I have worked hard to make the questionnaire easy to complete. For the most part you need only to read the question, check or circle the answer. However the section on COPING (beginning on page 7) is the heart of the research. Please select a single problem for that section and answer the following set of questions in relationship to what you did about that one problem. Please do not skip this section.

Please complete the questionnaire immediately. I have enclosed a self addressed stamped envelope to facilitate your reply. If you have questions regarding the study, you may call me at 415-569-0300, or Dr. Wilbur Finch at 213-743-8275, or the Institutional Review Board at 213-743-6781.

I will send you a summary of the results of my study. Just check the space at the end of the questionnaire.

Thank you so much for your help. Remember I can not do it without you.

Sincerely,

Lois Harry, Ph.D. Candidate
University of Southern California
School of Social Work

REFERENCES

Abram, H.S. (1970). *Psychological Aspects of Stress*. Springfield,Ill.: Charles C. Thomas.

Abramowitz, S.I. (1973). *Internal-External control and socialpolitical activism*. Journal of Consulting and Clinical Psychology, 40 (2), 196-201.

Abramson, P.R.(1977). *The Political Socialization of Black Americans*. New York: Free Press.

Adams, K.A. (1983). *Aspects of social context as determinants of black women's resistance to challenges*. Journal of Social Issues, 39 (3), 69-78.

Allen, W.R. (1979, Summer). *Family roles, occupational statuses, and achievement orientations among black women in the United States*. Signs: Journal of Women in Culture and Society, 4 (4), 670-686.

Allen, W.R. (1981, Spring). *The social and economic statuses of black women in the United States*. Phylon, 42, (1) 26-40.

Allen, W.R. (1986). *Black American Families* 1965-1984. New York: Greenwood Press.

Amott, T.L. & Matthaei, J.A.(1991). *Race, Gender, and Work*: A Multicultural Economic History of Women in the United States. Boston: South End Press.

Almquist, E.M. (1975). *Untangling the effects of race and sex: The disadvantaged status of black women*. Social Science Quarterly, 56, (1), 129-142.

Anderson, C.R. (1977). *Locus of control, coping behaviors, and performing in a stress setting: a longitudinal study*. Journal of Applied Psychology, 5, pp.3-16.

Andrews, E. (1986,January). *Running out of money*. Venture.pp. 32-35.

Appley, M. H. and Trumbull, R. (1967). *Psychological Stress: Issues in Research*. New York: Appleton-Century-Crofts.

Aspaklaria, S. (1986, March). *Down but not out*. Venture. PP. 58-60

Bailey, R.W.(ed).(1971). *Black Business Enterprise*. New York: Basic Books.

Bakalinsky, R. (1980, November). *People vs. Profits: Social work in industry*. Social Work.

Barbarin, 0. (1983). *Coping with ecological transitions by black families: a psychosocial model*. Journal of Community Psychology, 11, 308-322.

Barnes, A.S. (1981). *The black kinship system*, Phylon, 42 369-384.

Baruch, R. (1967). *The achievement motive in women: Implications for career development*. Journal of Personality and Social Psychology, 5 (3), 260-267.

Bass, B.A., Wyatt, G.E., Powell, G.J., (1982). *The Afro-American Family: Treatment and Research Issues*. New York: Grune and Stratton.

Baumgrardner, A. H., Heppner, P.P, and, Arkin, R.M. (1986). *Role of causal attribution in personal problem solving*. Journal of Personality and Social Psychology, 50, (3), 636-643.

Becker, B. and Tillman, F. (1978). *The Family Owned Business*. Chicago: Commerce Clearinghouse, Inc.

Benner, P.(1984). *Stress And Satisfaction On The Job*. New York: Praeger Press.

Blanchard-Fields, F. and Robinson, S.L. (1987). *Age differences in the relationship between controllability and coping*. Journal of Gerontology. 42, (5), 497-501.

Billings, A.G. and Moos, R.H. (1981). *The role of coping responses and social resources in attenuating the stress of life events*. Journal of Behavioral Medicine, 2, 139-157.

Billingsley, A. (1974). *Black Families And The Struggle For Survival*. New York: Friendship Press.

Billingsley, A. (1969,December). *Family functioning in the low income black community*. Social Casework.

Billingsley, A. (1968). *Black Families in White America*. Englewood Cliffs, N.J.: Prentice Hall.

Black, Pam. (1986, July). *A little help from her friends*. Venture, pp.52-58.

Black Entrepreneurship. (February 19, 1993).Wall Street Journal.Reports and Quarterly News Features, sec B.

Borland, C. (1975) *Locus of Control, Need for Achievement and Entrepreneurship*. Ann Arbor, Mich.: University Microfilms.

Boyd, R.L. *Black Entrepreneurship in 52 metropolitan areas*. Social Service Review. 75(3), pp.158-163.

Boyd, D. and Gumpert, D. (1983, March/April). *Coping with Entrepreneurial stress*. Harvard Business Review.

Brimmer, A. F. (1984, December). *Prosperity among black women*. Black Enterprise, p.45.

Brockhaus, Robert H. (1980). *Risk Taking Propensity of Entrepreneurs*. Academy of Management Journal, 37 (3), 509-520.

Brockhaus, R. and Horwitz,P.(1980) The psychology of the entrepreneur. in D. Sexton and R. Smilor (eds.). *The Art and Science of Entrepreneurship*. Cambridge, Mass.: Ballinger.

Brodhaus, R.H. (1984, April). *The effect of job dissatisfaction on the decision to start a business*. Journal of Small Business Management. pp.37-41.

Bromberg, W. (1975). *From Shaman to Psychotherapist.* Chicago: Henry Regnery Co.

Brown, B.(1984). *Between Health And Illness.* Boston: Houghton Muffin Co.

Brown, A., Goodwin, B.J., Hall, B.A., and Jackson-Lowman, H. (1985). *A review of psychology of women textbooks: Focus on the Afro-American woman.* Psychology of Women Quarterly, 9 (1), 29-39.

Brown, D.R. and Gary, L.E. (1985). *Social support network differential among married and non-married black females.* Psychology of Women Quarterly, 9, (3), 229-241.

Brown, T. (1968). *The color of freedom is green.* Black Perspectives, 3,(2), 1-5.

Bryant, Gay (ed.).(1984). *The Working Woman Report: Succeeding In Business In The 80's.* New York: Simon and Schuster.

Burack, E. H. (1984,April). *The sphinx riddle: Life and career cycles.* Training and Development Journal.

Bureau of the Census. (1979, June). *The Social and Economic Status of the Black Population in the United States: A Historical View* (Current Population Reports, Special Studies Series P-23 #80) Washington, D.C.: Department of Commerce

Burlew, A. K. (1982, Spring). *The experiences of black females in traditional and nontraditional professions.* Psychology of Women Quarterly, 6 (3), 312-325.

Burnham, L. (1985, March/April). *Has poverty been feminized in black America?* The Black Scholar, pp 145-24.

Bursch, J. *Entrepreneurship.*(1986). New York: Wiley and Sons.

Cade, T. (ed.).(1970). *The Black Woman.* New York: Mentor Books.

Case, F.E. (1972). *Black Capitalism: Problems in Development.* New York: Praeger.

Casson, M.(1982). *The Entrepreneur.* Totowa, N.J.: Barnes and Nobles.

Chestang, L. (1977). *Achievement And Self Esteem Among Blacks: A Study of Twenty Lives.* Ann Arbor, Mich.: University Microfilms International.

Chestang, L.W. (1984). *Racial and Personal Identity in the Black Experience.* In B.W. White (ed.) *Color in a White Society.* Silver Springs, Md.: National Association of Social Workers.

Coelho, G. and Ahmed, P.(1980). *Uprooting And Development: Dilemmas of Coping with Modernization.* New York: Plenum Press.

Cohen, S., Kamarch,T., and Mermelstein,R. (1983).*A global measure of perceived stress.* Journal of Health and Social Behavior, 24, 385-396.

Coleman,V.D. & Grothus-Magee, M.D.(1991). *Career assessment and development for female and minority entrepreneurs.* Man and Work, 3(1-2) pp. 82-92.

Coles, Jr., F., (1974). *The unique problems of the black businessman.* Review of Black Political Economy, 5, (1), 45-57.

Cooper, C.D. (1983). *Stress Research: Issues for the Eighties.* New York: John Wiley and Sons.

Cooper, C.L. (1981). *The Stress Check.* Englewood Cliffs, N.J.: Prentice-Hall.

Coyne, J.C. and Lazarus, R.S. (1980). *Cognitive style, stress perception, and coping.* In I. Kutash, L. Schlesinger and Associates (eds.). Handbook On Stress And Anxiety (pp. 144-158). San Francisco: Jossey-Bass.

Churchill, N.C. and Lewis, V.L. (1986). *Entrepreneurship research: Directions and methods.* In D.L. Sexton and R.W. Smilor (eds.). The Art and Science of Entrepreneurship. Cambridge, Mass.: Ballinger.

Cooper, C. (1982). *Executive Family Under Stress.* Englewood Cliffs, N.J.:Prentice-Hall.

Crost, J.C. (1984). *Successful turnarounds of independent businesses.* The Journal of Commercial Banking and Lending, 67(1), 28-39.

Crovitz, E. and Steinman,A. (1980). *A Decade later: Black-white attitudes toward women familial role.* Psychology of Women Quarterly, 5,(2), 170-176.

Curtin, R.T. (1982). *Running Your Own Show.* New York: John Wiley and Sons.

Cruse, H. (1967). *The Crisis Of The Negro Intellectual.* New York: William Morrow.

Davidson, M. and Cooper, C. (1983). *Stress And The Woman Manager.* New York: St. Martin Press.

Davis, P. Stern, D. (1980). *Adaptations, survival, and growth in the family business: A integrated system perspective.* Journal of Human Relations, 34 (1).

DeCarlo, J. and Lyons, P.R. (1979, December). *A comparison of selected characteristics of minority and non-minority female entrepreneurs.* Journal of Small Business Management, pp.22-29.

Delancy, A. (1979). *Black Task Force Report Project on Ethnicity.* New York: Family Service Association.

Depner, C.E. and Veroff, J. (1979). *Varieties of achievement motivation.* Journal of Social Psychology 107, 283-284.

Derogatis, L.R. (1982). *Self report measures of stress.* In L. Goldberger and S. Breznitz, Handbook of Stress. New York: Free Press.

Dingle, D. T. (1985, August). *New directions for black business.* Black EnterPrise.

Dingle, D.T. (1986, June). *Seeking an agenda for economic growth.* Black Enterprise.

Dingle, D. T. (1987, January). *Finding a prescription for black wealth.* Black Enterprise, pp. 39-48.

Dohrenwend, B.S. and Dohrenwend, B.P. (Eds.).(1974). *Stressful Life Events: Their Nature and Effects.* New York: Wiley.

Dolcher, L. (1982). *Effects of community and family background on achievement.* Review of Economics and Statistics, 64 (1), 32-41.

Donnelly, R. (1964). *The family business.* The Harvard Business Review, 42 (4).

Dream Deferred: The Economic Status of Black Americans (1984) Washington,D.C.: The center for the study of social policy.

Drucker, P.F. (1985). *Innovation And Entrepreneurship.* New York:Harper and Row.

Duffy, P.J., Shiflett, S., & Downey, R.G. (1977). *Locus of control: Dimensionality and predictability using Likert scales.* Journal of Applied Psychology, 62 (2), 214-219.

Dumas, L.S.(1993). *Do you think like an entrepreneur?.* Working Mother.pp.35-39.

Erikson, E. H.(1950). *Childhood and Society.* New York:Norton & Company.

Epstein, C.F. (1973). *Positive effects on the multiple negative:explaining the success of black professional women.* American Journal of Sociology, 78 (4), 912-935.

Feinberg, A.(1984, May). *Inside the entrepreneur.* Venture.

Ferguson, D. (1973). *A study of occupation, stress, and health.* Ergonomics, 16 (5), 649-663.

Flax, J. (1981). *A Materialist Theory of Womens's Status.* Psychology of Women Quarterly, 6, (1), 123-135.

Fleishman, J.A. (1984). *Personality, characteristics, and coping patterns.* Journal of Health and Social Behavior, 25, 229-244.

Fleming, J. (1982). *Fear of Success in black male and female graduate students: A pilot study.* Psychology of Women Quarterly, 6, (3), 327-341.

Folkman, S. *Personal control and stress and coping process: A theoretical analysis.* Journal of Personality and Social Psychology, 56, (4), 839-852.

Folkman, S. and Lazarus, R.S. (1980). *An analysis of coping in a middle-aged community sample.* Journal of Health and Social Behavior, 21, 219-239.

Folkman,S. and Lazarus, R.S. (1985). *If it changes it must be a process: study of emotion and coping during three stages of a college examination.* Journal of Personality and Social Psychology, 48 (1), 150-170.

Folkman, S., Lazarus, R.S., Dunkel-Schetter, C., Delongis, A., and Gruen, R.J.(1986). *Dynamics of a stressful encounter: cognitive appraisal, coping and encounter outcomes.* Journal Of Personality and Social Psychology, 50 (5), 992-1003.

Folkman, S., Lazarus, R.S., Gruen, R.J., & Delongis, A. (1986). *Appraisal, coping, health status, and psychological symptoms.* Journal of Personality and Social Psychology, 50 (3), 571-579.

Frank, D. (1972). *Persuasion and Healing.* Baltimore: John Hopkins University Press.

Frazier, E.F.(1957). *The Black Bourgeoisie.* New York: Free Press.

Frazier, E.F. (1966). *The Negro Family in the United States.* Chicago:Chicago University Press.

Frey,B.R. & Noller, R.B.(1986). *Mentoring: A promise for the future.* Journal of Creative Behavior, 20 (1) pp. 49-51.

Fucini, J. and Fucini, S. (1985). *Entrepreneurs.* Boston: G.K. Hall and Co.

Furenstenberg, F.F., Jr., Hershberg, T., and Modell, J. (1975). *The origin of the female headed black family: The impact of the urban experience.* Journal of Interdisciplinary History, 6,(2), 211-233.

Furnham, A.(1989). *Communicating across cultures: a social skills perspective.* Counselling Psychology Quarterly, 2 (2),pp. 205-222.

Gaston, J.C. (1980). *The acculturation of the first generation of black professional women: A Denver, Colorado area study.* The Western Journal of Black Studies, 4 (4), 256-260.

Gibbs, J.T. (1984). *Conflicts and coping strategies of minority female graduate students.* In B.W. White (ed.) Color in a White Society (pp. 22-36). Silver Springs, Md.- National Association of Social Workers, Inc.

Giddings, P. (1984). *When and Where I Enter.* New York: Bantam.

Gilkes, C. T. (1982). *Successful rebellious professionals: The black woman's professional identity and community.* Psychology of Women Quarterly, 6 (3), 289-311.

Gillespie, M.A. (1984). *The myth of the strong black woman.* In A.M. Jaggar and P.S. Rothenberg (eds.) Feminist Frameworks.(2nd Ed.). (pp.32-35). New York: McGraw-Hill.

Ginberg, E. (1968). *The Middle Class Negro In The White Man's World.* New York:Columbia Press.

Goldberger, L. and Breznitz, S. (1982). *Handbook of Stress.* New York: Free Press.

Googin, B. and Godfrey, J (1985, September/October). *The evolution of occupational social work.* Social Work.

Gould, S.J. (1981). *The Mismeasure of Man.* New York: Norton.

Graves, E. (1982,August/September). *Black buying power: a sizable force in the market.* Crisis.

Greiff, B.S. and Munter, P.K.(1980). *Tradeoffs: Executive, Family and Organization.* Life. New York: Mentor Books.

Greenfield, S.M., Strickon, A., and Aubrey, R.T. (1979). *Entrepreneurs in cultural context.* Albuquerque: University of New Mexico Press.

Grier, W.H. and Cobbs P.M. (1971). *The Jesus Bag*. New York: McGraw-Hill.

Griffin, J.T. (1986). *Black woman's experiences as authority figures in groups*. Women's Studies Quarterly, 14 (1&2), 7-12.

Griffith, E.E.H., Young, J.L., and Smith, D. L.(1984). *An analysis of the therapeutic elements of a black church service*. Hospital and Community Psychiatry, 35 (5), 464-473.

Grisante, D. and Gumpert, D. (1982, November/December). *The agony of selling out to relatives*. Harvard Business Review.

Guagnano, G., Acredolo, C., Hawkes, G.R., Ellyson, S., & White, N.(1987). *Locus of Control: Demographic factors and their interactions*. Journal of Social Behavior and Personality.1 (3), pp. 356-380.

Gump. J.P. (1975). *Comparative analysis of black and white womens' sex role attitudes*. Journal of Consulting and Clinical Psychology, 43 (6), 858-863.

Gump, J.P. (1978). *Reality and myth: Employment and role ideology in black women*. In J. A. Sherman L. Denmark (eds.) Psychology of Women: Future Directions in Research. (pp. 349-380). New York. Psychological Dimensions.

Gurin, P. Gurin, G. Lao, R. and Beattre, M. (1972). *Internal-external control in the motivational dynamics of negro youth*. In S.S. Guterman (ed.) Black Psyche-The Modal Personality Patterns in Black America. Berkeley, Ca. The Glendessary Press, Inc.

Gutman, H.G. (1976). *The Black Family in Slavery and Freedom 1750-1925*. New York: Vintage Books.

Gynther, M.D., Lachar, D., & Dahlstrom, W.G. (1978). *Are special norms for minorities needed?* Development of a MMPI F scale for blacks. Journal of Consulting and Clinical Psychology, 46(6),pp.1403-1408.

Haggerty, R.J. (1983). *Foreword*. in N.Garmezy and Rutter.(eds.). Stress, Coping and Development in Children. New York. McGraw-Hill.

Hare, N. and Hare, J. (1984). *The Endangered Black Family: Coping with the Unisexualization and Coming Extinction of the Black Race*. San Francisco: Black Think Tank.

Harely, S. and Terborg-Penn, R. (eds). (1978). *The Afro-American woman: Struggles and Images*. Port Washington, N.Y.: Kennihat Press.

Harlan, S.L.(1985). *Federal job training policy and economically disadvantaged women*. in L.Larwood, A.H. Stromberg, & B.A.Gutek (eds.).Women and Work: An Annual Review. Vol.1(pp. 282-310).Newbury Park, CA: Sage.

Harrison, A.O. and Minor, J.H. (1982). *Interrole conflict, coping strategies and role satisfaction among single and married employed mothers*. Psychology of Women Quarterly, 6,(3), 4-361.

Harrison, P. (1986). *America's New Women Entrepreneurs.*
Washington, D.C.: Accopolis Books, Ltd.

Harrison, S.S. (1988, August). *Across the board.* Black Enterprise,
46-52.

Hartman, C. (1985, July). *The spirit of independence.* Inc. (pp. 47-91).

Herman, A.M. (1984). *Still...Small change for black women.* In A.M.
Jaggar and P.S. Rothenberg. Feminist Frameworks. (2nd Ed.).
(pp.36-40). New York-McGraw-Hill.

Higgs, R. (1977). *Competition and Coercion: Blacks in The American
Economy 1865-1914.* Cambridge, Mass.: Cambridge University
Press.

Hill, R. (1977). *Racism and Mental Health.* Pittsburgh: University of
Pittsburgh Press.

Hisrich, R.D. (1986). *The woman entrepreneur: Characteristics, skills,
problems, and prescriptions for success.* in D. Sexton and R.
Smilor (eds.). The Art and Science of
Entrepreneurship.Cambridge, Mass.: Ballinger.

Hisrich, R.D.(1986). *The woman entrepreneur: A comparative analysis.*
Leadership and Organization Development Journal, 7(2), pp 8-16.

Hisrich, R.D. and Brush, C. G.(1985). *Women and minority
entrepreneurs: a comparative analysis.* in K.H. Vesper(ed.).
Frontiers of Entrepreneurship Research. Wellesley, Mass.:
Babson Center for Entrepreneurial Studies.

Hisrich, R.D. and Brush, C.G. (1984, January). *The woman
entrepreneur: management skills and business problems.* Journal
of Small Business Management.

Hoffman, L.W. (1972). *Early childhood experiences and Women's
achievement motives.* Journal of Social Issues, 28(2), 129-156.

Holdorf, P. M. (1983). *Stress and Role Relationships in An
Organization: A Study in Coping Behaviors.* Ann Arbor, Mich.:
University Microfilms International.

Holland, P. and Bouton, W.(1984, March/April). *Balancing the
"family" and the "business' in the family business.* Business
Horizons.

Holmes, T.H. and Rahe, R.H. (1967). *The social adjustment rating
scale.* Journal of Psychosomatic Research, 11, 213-218.

Holroyd, K.A. and Lazarus, R.S. (1982). *Stress, coping, and somatic
adaptation.* in L. Goldberger and S. Breznitz (eds.).Handbook of
Stress.(pp. 21-35). New York: Free Press.

Hooks, B. (1984). *The myth of black matriarchy.* In A.M. Jaggar and
P.S. Rothenberg. Feminist Frameworks. (2nd ed.).(pp. 369-373).
New York: McGraw-Hill.

Hornaday, J.A. and Bunker. C.S. (1970). *The nature of the
entrepreneur.* Personnel Psychology, 23, 47-54.

Hornaday, J. A. and Aboud, J. (1971). *Characteristics of successful
entrepreneurs.* Personnel Psychology, 24, 141-153.

Horner, M.S. (1972). *Toward an understanding of achievement-related conflicts in women*. Journal of Social Issues, 28 (2), 157-175.

House Committee on Small Business. *New Economic Realities: The Rise of Women Entrepreneurs*. report prepared by John A. LaFalce, 100 Cong.,2d sess.,1988, Report 100-736.

Howell, D. (1986, April/May). *The psychology of black economics*. Black Perspectives.

Howell, E. and Boyce, M. (eds.). (1981). *Women and Mental Health*. New York: Basic Books.

Hull, G. T., Scott, P. B., Smith, B. (1982). *But Some of Us are Brave*. Old Westbury, N.Y.: The Feminist Press.

Hund, J.M. (1970). *Black Entrepreneurship*. Belmont. Ca.: Wadsworth.

Hylton, R. D. (1988, August). *Working in America*. BlackEnterprise, pp. 63-66.

Irion, J.C. and Blanchard-Fields, F. (1987). *A cross-sectional comparison of adaptive coping in adulthood*. Journal of Gerontology 42 (5), 502-504.

Jeffers, T. (1981). *The black woman and the black middle class*. The Black Scholar, 12, (6), 46-49.

Jenkins, A. (1982). *The Psychology of the Afro-American*. New York: Peragmon.

Johnson, P.L. (1985) *The black entrepreneur*. Crisis, 92 (2), 16-21, 46-48.

Jones E.H. (1971). *Blacks in Business*. New York: Grosset and Dunlap.

Jones, T.F. (1987). *Entrepreneurism*. New York: Donald Fine, Inc.

Kamii, C. and Radin, N. (1967). *Class differences in socialization practices of negro families*. Journal of Marriage and Family, 80 (2), 302-310.

Kanter, R. (1976). *Work and The Family in The United States*. New York: Russell Sage Foundation.

Kaplan, H.B. (1983). *Psychological distress in sociological context: toward a general theory of psychosocial stress*. In H.B. Kaplan (ed.). Psychosocial Stress (pp. 195-266). New York: Academic Press.

Kaplan, H.B.(1983). *Psychosocial Stress: Trends in Theory and Research*. New York: Academic Press.

Karenga, M. (1982). *The crisis of black middle class leadership: a critical analysis*. The Black Scholar, 13(6), 16-36.

Kent, C.A. (1984). *The Environment for Entrepreneurship*. Lexington, Ma.: Lexington Press.

Kerlinger, F. N. (1973). *Foundations of Behavioral Research* (2nd Edition). New York: Holt, Rinehart, and Winston.

Kets de Vries, M.F.R. (1985, November/December). *The dark side of entrepreneurship*. Harvard Business Review.

Kets de Vries, M.F.R.(1977, February). *The entrepreneurial personality: a person at the crossroads*. The Journal of Management Studies (pp.34-57).

Kilby, P. (1971). *Entrepreneurship and Economic Development*. New York: Free Press.

Kilson, M. (1981). *Politics and identity among black intellectuals*. Dissent, 28, 339-349.

King, S. R. (1988, March). *Back from the brink*. Black Enterprise, pp 40-46.

King, S. R. (1988, August). *Black women in corporate america at the crossroads*. Black Enterprise, pp. 45-56.

Kinkhead, G. (1980, June 30). *Family business is a passion play*. Fortune, Kobasa, S.C., Maddi, S.R., and Courington,S. (1981). Personality and constitution as mediators in the stress-illness relationship. Journal of Health and Social Behavior, 22, 368-78.

Kobasa, S.C. Maddi,S.R. and Zola, M.A. (1983). *Type A and hardiness*. Journal of Behavioral Medicine 6 (1), 41-51.

Koenig, H.G., Kale, J.N., and Ferrel, C. (1988). *Religion and well-being in later life*. The Gerontologist, 28,(1), 18-27.

Kohut, H.(1971). *The Analysis of the Self*. New York: International University Press.

Kohut, H. (1977). *Restoration of the Self*. New York: International University Press.

Kurzman, P. and Akabas, S. (1981). *Industrial social work as an arena of practice*. Social Work, 26 (1).

Kutash, I.L., & Schlesinger, L. (1980). *Handbook on Stress and Anxiety*. San Francisco: Jossey-Bass Publishers.

Ladner, J.A. (1971). *Tomorrow's Tomorrow: The BlackWoman*. Garden City. N.Y.: Doubleday.

Landis, P. H. (1964). *Sociology*. Boston: Ginn and Company.

Landry, B. (1987). *The New Black Middle Class*. Berkeley, CA. University of California Press.

Landry, B. and Jendrick, M.P. (1978). *The employment of wives in middle class black families*. Journal of Marriage and Family, 40, (4), 787-797.

La Rocco, J.M., House, J. S. and French, J.R.P. (1980). *Social support, occupational stress, and health*. Journal of Health and Social Behavior, 21, 202-218.

Larson, C. and Chute, R. (1978, November). *The failure syndrome*. American Journal of Small Business.

Latting, J.E. and Zundel, C. (1986). *World View Differences between clients and counselors*. Social Casework, 67, (9), 533-541.

Lazarus, R.S. (1981). *The stress and coping paradigm*. in C. Eisdorfer et.al. Models for Clinical Psycho-pathology. New York: S.P. Medical and Scientific Books.

Lazarus, R.S. (1982). *The psychology of stress and coping.* in C. Spielberger and I.S. Sarason (eds.). Stress and Anxiety, 8, 23-36.

Lazarus, R.S., Averill, J. and Opton, E. (1974). *The psychology of coping: Issues, research, and assessment.* in G.V. Coelho, D.A.Hamburg, and J.E. Adams. Coping and Adaptation. New York: Basic Books.

Lazarus. R.S. and Launier, R. (1978). *Stress-related transactions between person and environment.* in L.A. Pervin and M. Lewis (eds.). Perspectives in Interfactional Psychology (pp.287-327).New York: Plenum Press.

Lazarus, R.S. and Folkman, S. (1984). *Stress, Appraisal, and Coping.* New York: Springer Press.

Ledsock, S. (1984). *The Free Women of Petersburg.* New York: W.W.Norton.

Lefcourt, H. (1976). *Locus of control.* Hillsdale, N.J.: Lawrence Erlebaum Associates.

Lefcourt, H. M., Miller, R.S., Ware, E.E., and Sherk, D. (1981). *Locus of control as a modifier of the relationship between stressors and moods.* Journal of Personality and Social Psychology, 41 (2), 357-369.

Lefcourt, H.M. and Ladwig, G.W. (1964). *The American negro: A problem in expectancies.* Journal of Personality and Psychology, 1, (4), 377-330.

Levenson, H. (1973a). *Multidimensional locus of control in psychiatric patients.* Journal of Consulting and Clinical Psychology, 41(3), 397-404.

Levenson, H. (1973b). *Perceived parental antecedents of internal, powerful others, and chance locus of control orientations.* Developmental Psychology, 9 (2), 268-274.

Levenson, H. (1974). *Activism and powerful others: distinctions within the concept of internal-external control.* Journal of Personality Assessment, 38, 377-383.

Levenson, H. (1975). *Additional dimensions of internal-external Locus of control.* Journal of Social Psychology, 97, 303-304.

Lewis, D.K. (1977). *A response to inequality: Black women, racism, and sexism.* Journal of Women in Culture and Society, 3, (2), 339-361.

Lewis, J. and Looney, J. (1983). *The Long Struggle: Well Functioning Working Class Black Families.* New York: Bruker/Mazel Publishers.

Liebow, E. (1967). *Tally's Corner.* Boston: Brown and Company.

Light, I.H. (1972). *Ethnic Enterprise in America: Business and Welfare Among Chinese, Japanese, and Blacks.* Berkeley: University of California Press.

Lincoln, Y.S. (1985). *Organizational Theory and Inquiry: The Paradigm Revolution*. Beverly Hills, Ca.: Sage Publications.

Loden, M. (1985). *Feminine Leadership or How to Succeed in Business without being one of the Boys*. New York: Times Books.

Long, W. (1983). *The meaning of entrepreneurship*. American Journal of Small Business, 8, (2), 47-56 59.

Lowrey, R. (1973). *Dominance, Self-Esteem and Self-Actualization*. Germinal Papers of A. H. Maslow. Monterey, Ca.: Brooks/Cole Publishing Co.

Lykes, M.B. (1983). *Discrimination and coping in the lives of black women: Analysis of oral history data*. Journal of Social Issues, 39 (3), 79-100.

Maddi, S.R., and Kobasa,S. (1984). *The Hardy Executive*. Homewood, Ill.: Dow Jones-Irwin.

Malson, M. R. (1983) *Black Women's Sex Roles: The social context for a new ideology*. Journal of Social Issues, 39 (3), 101-113.

Manuso, J. (1983). *Occupational Clinical Psychology*. New York: Praeger Publishers.

Marable, M. (1983). *How Capitalism Underdeveloped Black America*. Boston: South End Press.

Martin, E.P. and Martin, J.M. (1971). *The Black Extended Family*. Chicago: University of Chicago Press.

Martin, J.K. & Hall, G.C.N.(1992). *Thinking black, thinking internal, thinking feminist*.Journal of Counseling Psychology, 39(4), 509-514.

Martin, J. and Martin, E. (1985). *The Helping Tradition in the Black Family and Community*. Silver Spring, Md.: NASW.

Mays, V. M. (1985). *Black women working together: Diversity in some sex relationships*. Women's Studies International Forum, 8 (1), 67-71.

Mbiti, J. S. (1970). *African Religions and Philosophy*. Garden City, N.Y.: Anchor Books.

McAdoo, H. P. (1981). *Black Families*. Beverly Hills, Ca.: Sage Press.

McAdoo, H. P. (1982). *Demographic trends for people of color*. Social Work, 27 (1).

McEvoy, G. M. (1983). *Personnel practices in smaller firms: A survey and recommendations*. American Journal of Small Business, 8 (2), 32-46.

McClelland, D. C. (1961). *The Achieving Society*. Princeton: Van Nostrand.

McClelland, D. C. (1965). *Achievement and entrepreneurship*. Journal of Personality and Social Psychology, 1 (4), 389-392.

McCrae, R.R. (1984). *Situational determinants of coping responses: loss, threat, and challenge*. Journal of Personality and Social Psychology, 46 (4), 919-928.

McLean, A.A. (1979). *Work Stress*. Reading, Ma.: Addison-Wesley.

Mead, G.H. (1934). *Mind, Self, and Society*. Chicago: University of Chicago Press.

Meltzer, M. (1970). *In Their Own Words: A History of the American Negro*. New York: Thomas Y. Crowell.

Menaghan, E.G. (1983). *Individual coping efforts: moderators of the relationship between life stress and mental health outcomes*. in H.W. Kaplan (ed.). Psychosocial stress (pp. 157-191). New York: Academic Press.

Minkwitz, E.G. (1967). *The Negro in American Life and History*. San Francisco: San Francisco Unified School District.

Mirels, H. (1970). *Dimensions of internal versus external control*. Journal of Consulting and Clinical Psychology, 34 (2), 226-228.

Monat, A. and Lazarus, R.S. (eds). (1976). *Stress and Coping*. New York: Columbia University Press.

Moore, L.L. (1986). *Not As Far As You Think*. Lexington, Ma: Lexington Books.

Moos, R.H. and Billings, A.G. (1982). *Conceptualizing and measuring coping resources and processes*. in L. Goldberger and S. Breznitz (eds.). Handbook of Stress: Theoretical and Clinical Aspects (pp. 212-230). New York: Free Press.

Moss, L. (1981). *Management Stress*. Reading, Mass.: Addison-Wesley Publishing Co.

Moses, Y.T. (1985). *Black American women and work: Historical and contemporary strategies for empowerment-II*. Women's Studies International Forum, 8(4), 351-359.

Myers, L. W. (1980). *Black Women: Do They Cope Better?* Englewood Cliffs, N.J.: Prentice-Hall, Inc.

Murray, S.R. and Harrison, D.D. (1981). *Black Women and the Future*. Psychology of Women Quarterly, 6(1), 113-122.

Murray, S.R., Medneck, M. and Schuch, T. (1977). *Black women's achievement orientation: Motivational and cognitive factors*. Psychology of Women Quarterly, 1(3), 247-259.

Murphy, L. and Moriarity, A. (1976). *Vulnerability, Coping, and Growth: From Infancy to Adolescence*. New Haven: Yale University Press.

Myrdal, G. (1962). *An American Dilemma: The Negro Problem and Modern Democracy*. New York: Harper and Row.

Neff, J.A. (1985). *Race and vulnerability to stress: an examination of differential vulnerability*. Journal of Personality and Social Psychology, 49(2), 481-491.

Neighbors, H. W., Jackson, J.S., and Bowman, B.J.(1983). *Stress, coping, and black mental health: Preliminary findings from a national study*. Prevention in Human Services, 2 (3), 5-29.

Nezu, A.M. and Ronan, G.F. (1985). *Life stress, current problems, and depressive symptoms: an integrative model*. Journal of Consulting and Clinical Psychology, 53 (5), 693-697.

Nichalls, J. G. (1975). *Causal attributes and other achievement related cognitions: effects of task outcome, attainment value and sex.* Journal of Personality and Social Psychology, 31 (3), 379-389.

Noble, B. P. (1986, July). *A sense of self.* Venture pp. 34-36.

Noble, J.L. (1978). *Beautiful, Also, Are The Souls of My Black Sisters: A History of Black Women in America.* Englewood Cliffs, N.J.: Prentice-Hall.

Odioine, G. (1978, April). *Executives under siege.* Management Review, 67.

Okazawa-Rey, M., Robinson, T., and Ward, J. V., (1986). *Black women and the politics of skin color and hair.* Women's Studies Quarterly, 14 (1 & 2) 13-14.

Olm, K. and Eddy, G. (1985). *Entrepreneurship and Venture Management.* New York: Charles E. Merrill.

Olson, P. and Basserman, J. (1984). *Attributes of the Entrepreneurial Types.* Business Horizons, 27 (3).

Padilla, A.M. (1980). *Acculturation: Theory, Models, and Some New Findings.* Boulder. Colo.: Westview Press.

Palmer, P. (1983). *The racial feminization of Poverty: Women of color as portents of the future of all women.* Women's Studies Quarterly, 11 (3), 4-6.

Pardine, P. et.al.(1981). *Job stress, worker-strain relationship, moderated by the off the job experience.* Psychological Reports, 48, 963-970.

Parker. S. Kleiner, R. (1966). *Mental Illness in The Urban Negro Community.* New York: Free Press.

Parkes, K.R. (1984). *Locus of control, cognitive appraisal and coping in stressful episodes.* Journal of Personality and Social Psychology, 46 (3), 655-668.

Pearlin, L.I. and Schooler, C. (1978). *The structure of coping.* Journal of Health and Social Behavior, 19, 2-21.

Pearlin, L.I., Lieberman, M.A., Menaghan, E.G., and Mullan, J.T. (1981). *The stress process.* Journal of Health and Social Behavior, 22, 337-356.

Pearlin, L.I. (1983). *Role strain and personal stress.* in H.B. Kaplan (ed.). Psychosocial Stress. New York: Academic Press.

Pellegrino, E. T. and Reece, B.L. (1982, April). *Perceived formative and operational problems encountered by female entrepreneurs in retail and service firms.* Journal of Small Business Management.

Pelletier, K. (1982). *Healthy People in Unhealthy Places: Stress and Fitness at Work.* Merloyd Lawrence, N.Y.: Delacorte Press.

Peters, T. and Waterman, R. (1982). *In Search of Excellence.* New York: Warner Books.

Pines, M. (1980, December). *Psychological Hardiness.* Psychology Today, 34-44, 98.

Poussaint, R. (1985, February). *What happens when a black "first" fails?* Ms p.84

Puryearr, G.R. and Medneck, M.S. (1974). *Black militancy, affective attachment, and the fear of success in black college women.* Journal of Consulting and Clinical Psychology, 42 (2), 263-266.

Rainwater, L. (1967). *The Moynihan Report and the Politics of Controversy.* Cambridge, Mass.: M.I.T.Press.

Richman, T. (1985, April). *Personal business.* Inc.

Rodgers-Rose, L. (ed.).(1980). *The Black Woman.* Beverly Hills, Ca.: Sage.

Ronstadt, R.C. (1981). *Entrepreneurial careers and research on entrepreneurs.* in K.H. Vesper (ed.).Frontiers on Entrepreneurship Research. Wellesley, Mass.: Babson Center for Entrepreneurial Studies.

Rotter, J.B. (1966). *Generalized expectancies for internal versus external control of reinforcement.* Psychological Monographs, 80, Whole No. 609.

Rotter, J. B. (1971, June). *External control and internal control.* Psychology Today, pp. 38-42, 58-59.

Rotter, J.B. (1975). *Some problems and misconceptions related to the construct of internal versus external control of reinforcement.* Journal of Consulting and Clinical Psychology 43,(1), 56-67.

Russell, M. and Lyston, M.J. (1984). *Black women and the market.* In A.M. Jaggar and P.S. Rothenberg (eds.).Feminist Frameworks.(2nd ed.).New York: McGraw-Hill.

Russell, S. (1984, May). *Being your own boss in America.* Venture.

Rutter, M. (1983). *Stress, coping, and development: some issues and some questions.* in N. Garmezy and M. Rutter (eds.). Stress, Coping and Development in Children. New York: McGraw-Hill.

Ryan, W. (1971). *Blaming The Victim.* New York: Vintage Books.

Sanchez, C.L. (1983). *Racism: Power, profit, product, and patriarchy.* Women's Studies Quarterly, 11,(3), 14-16.

Scanzoni, J. H. (1971). *The Black Family in Modern Society.* Boston: Allyn and Bacon, Inc.

Scheinfeld, D. (1983, January). *Family relationships and school achievement among lower income urban black families.* American Journal of Orthopsychiatry.

Schulz, D. (1969). *Coming Up Black.* Englewood, N.J.: Prentice Hall, Inc.

Schwartz, E. B. (1976, Winter). *Entrepreneurship: a new female frontier.* Journal of Contemporary Business. pp. 47-76.

Selye, H. (1956). *The Stress of Life.* New York: McGraw-Hill.

Selye, H. (1974). *Stress without Distress.* Philadelphia: Lippincott Co.

Selye, H. (1982). *History and status of the stress concept*. In L. Goldberger and S. Breznitz. (eds.). Handbook of Stress: Theoretical and Clinical Aspects. (pp. 7-20). New York: Free Press.

Seglin, J. L.(1985, July). *Growing by their bootstraps*. Venture.

Sexton, D. and Smilor, R. (1986). *The Art and Science of Entrepreneurship*. Cambridge, Mass.: Ballinger Co.

Silver, A. D. (1983). *The Entrepreneurial Life*. New York: John Wiley and Sons.

Simpson, J.H. (1980). *Survival of minorities in the labor market*. Social Perspectives, 7, (1), 20-29.

Smith, A.and Stewart, A.J. (1983). *Approaches to studying racism and sexism in black women's lives*. Journal of Social Issues, 39, (3), 1-15.

Smith, A.W.(1987). *Racial trends and countertrends in american organizational behavior*. Journal of Social Issues, 43,(1) pp. 91-94.

Smith, B. (ed.).(1983). *Home Girls*. New York: Kitchen Table:Women of Color Press.

Smith, E. (1985). *Black american women and work: a historical review 1619-1920*. Women's Studies International Forum, 8, (4), 343-349.

Smith, E.J. (1981). *Mental health and service delivery systems for black women*. Journal of Black Studies, 12,(2), 126-141.

Smith, E.J. (1982). *The black female adolescent: A review of the educational and psychological literature*. Psychology of Women Quarterly, 6,(3), 261-287.

Smith E.J. and Smith, P.M., Jr. (1986). *The black female single-parent family condition*. Journal of Black Studies, 17(1),125-134.

Smith, A.W.(1987). *Racial Trends and Countertrends in American Organization Behavior*. Journal of Social Issues.43,(1) pp. 91-44.

Smith, N.R. (1967). *The Entrepreneur and His Firm: The Relationship Between the Type of Man and the Type of Company*. East Lansing, Mi.: Michigan State University.

Snyder, C. Manz, C., and Forge, R. (1983). *Self management: A key to entrepreneurial survival*. American Journal of Small Business, 8(1).

Solomon, B.B. (1976). *Black Empowerment: Social Work in Oppressed Communities*. New York: Columbia University.

Stack, C. (1974). *All Our Kin*. New York: Harper and Row.

Staples, R. (1973). *The Black Woman in America*. Chicago: Nelson Hall.

Staples, R. (1984,0ctober). *The mother-son relationship in the black family*. Ebony.

State of Black America. (1982). New York: Urban League.

Stephenson, H. B. (1984). *The most critical problem of the fledgling small business: getting sales*. American Journal of Small Business, 9(1).

Stewart, A. J.(1978). *A longitudinal study of coping styles in self-defining and socially defined women.* Journal of Consulting and Clinical Psychology, 46(5), 1079-1084.

Strauss, A. (1972). *George Herbert Mead on Social Psychology.* Chicago: University of Chicago Press.

Subira, G. (1986). *Black Folks Guide to Business.* Newark, N.J.:Very Serious Business Enterprise.

Sue, D.W. (1978). *Eliminating cultural oppression in counseling: Toward a general theory.* Journal of Counseling Psychology, 25(5), 419-428.

Sullivan, T.A.& McCracken, S.D.(1988). *Black entrepreneurs: Patterns and rates of return to self-employment.* National Journal of Sociology.pp. 167-185.

Swan, L.A. (1981). *Survival and Progress: the Afro-American Experience.* Westport, Conn.: Greenwood Press.

Sykes, D. K. (1985). *Effects of sex and race on the vocational aspiration of third and fifth grade children.* School Social Work Journal, 9(2), 144-155.

Synder, C., Manz, C. and La Forge, R. (1983). *Self management: a key to entrepreneurial survival.* Journal of Small Business 8 (1).

Tashakkori, A. & Thompson, V.D.(1991). *Racial differences in self-perspection and locus of control during adolescence and early adulthood.* Methodological Implications. Genetic, Social and General Psychology Mongraphs, 117(2), 153-174.

Thompson, K. D. (1988, August) *Starting Over.* Black Enterprise. pp. 58-61.

Timmons, J. (1980). *Characteristics and role demands of entrepreneurs.* American Journal of Small Business, 4(3).

Torrance, E. P. (1965). *Constructive Behavior.* Belmont. Ca.: Wadsworth Publishing Co.

U.S. Bureau of the Census. (1988). *Statistical Abstracts of the United States (108th Edition).* Washington, D.C.: Department of Commerce.

U.S. Bureau of Census. (1979). *The Social and Economic Status of the Black Population in the United States: A Historical View, 1790-1978.* Washington, D.C.: Department of Commerce.

U. S. Commission on Civil Rights. (1983, May). *A Growing Crisis: Disadvantaged Women and Their Children.* (Publication #78). Washington, D.C.: Clearinghouse.

U.S. Department of Labor, Women's Bureau.(1989). *American indian/alaska native women business owners.* Facts on Working Women. No.89-9

U.S. Department of Labor, Women's Bureau.(1989). *Asian american women business owners.* Facts on Working Women. No. 89-8.

U.S. Department of Labor, Women's Bureau.(1992). *Women workers: outlook to 2005.* Facts on Working Women. No.92-1.

U.S. Department of Labor, Women's Bureau.(1989). *Black women businessowners*. Facts on Working Women. No. 89-7.

U.S. Department of Labor, Women's Bureau.(1990). *Black women in the labor Force*. Facts on Working Women. No.90-4.

Valentine, B. (1978). *Hustling and Other Hard Work*. New York: Free Press.

Vatter, H. and Palm, T. (1972). *The Economics of Black America*. New York:Harcourt, Brace,& Javanovich, Inc.

Villemez, W. J. and Beggs, J. J. (1984). *Black capitalism and black inequality: some sociological considerations*.Social Forces, 63,(1).

Wallace, R. A. (1980). *Black Women in the Labor Force*. Cambridge, Mass: The MIT Press.

Watson, P. (1973). *Psychology and Race*. Baltimore: Penguin Press.

Weinrauch, J.D. (1984, April). *Educating the entrepreneur: Understanding adult learning behavior*. Journal of Small Business Management.

Weick, A. and Pope, L. (1988). *Knowing what's best: a new look at self-determination*. Social Work, 69 (1), 10-16.

Weiner, H. D. (1979). *Cognitive theory*. In F.J. Turner (ed.). Social Work Treatment: Interlocking Theoretical Approaches.New York: Free Press.

Wheaton, B. (1985). *Models for the stress buffering functions of coping resources*. Journal of Health and Social Behavior, 26, 352-364.

White, B. W. (ed.). (1982). *Color in a White Society*. Silver Springs, Md.:National Association of Social Workers, Inc.

Wilcox, R.C. (1977). *The Psychological Consequences of Being a Black American*. New York: John Wiley and Sons.

Wilkens, J. (1987). *Her Own Business: Success Secrets of Entrepreneurial Woman*. New York: McGraw-Hill.

Willhelm, S. M. (1986). *The economic demise of blacks in America*. Journal of Black Studies, 17 (2), 201-254.

Willie, C. (1970). *The Family Life of Black People*. Columbus, Ohio: CharlesMerrill.

Willie, C. (1981). *A New Look at Black Families*. Bayside, N.Y.: General Hall, Inc.

Willie, C. V., Kramer, B. M., and Brown, B. S. (eds.).(1973). *Racism and Mental Health*. Pittsburgh, Pa.; University of Pittsburgh.

Wortman, M. S. (1986). *A unified research topologies and research prospective for the interface between entrepreneurship and the small business*. In D.L. Sexton and R.W. Smilor (eds.). The Art and Science of Entrepreneurship. Cambridge. Mass.: Balliner.

Women at work *"Research Spotlights"* (1978, November) Management Review.

Young, W. (1964). *To Be Equal*. New York: McGraw-Hill.

Zollar, A. (1985). *A Member of the Family*: Strategies for Black Family Continuity. Chicago: Nelson-Hall.

INDEX